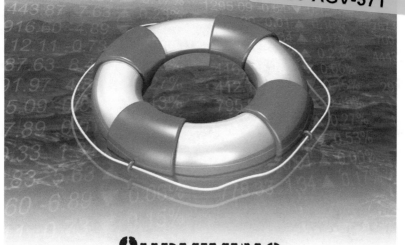

SURVIVING THE PERFECT RECESSION

How to take control of your career and improve
your finances during the worst economic downturn
since the Great Depression

DR. STEVE W. PRICE

METAPHOR
PRESS

Surviving the Perfect Recession
by Dr. Steve W. Price

Metaphor Press
10427 Orange Grove Dr.
Tampa, FL 33618

Distributed exclusively through:
High Mountain Marketing
140 S. Main Street
Brooksville, FL 34601

ISBN: 978-0-9822549-1-2
Published by Metaphor Press

Printed in United States of America

Cover design and text layout by Parry Design Studio, Inc.

Read This First!

The Difference between Being Negative and Being Real

> *A pessimist is someone who, when he smells flowers, looks around for the casket.*
> —H.L. Mencken

I don't particularly like people who are negative—people who think there's a worm in every apple or a disaster in every dream.

On the other hand, I do like people who are *real*—people who will tell it to you straight, even if it's bad news.

If someone goes to the doctor complaining about chest pain, and the doctor correctly diagnoses a heart attack, the doctor isn't being negative. He's just being real. No sense skirting the issue if the reality is serious. Best to lay out the facts, call in a cardiologist, diagnose the causes of the heart attack, and recommend a treatment plan that will get the patient back on the road to recovery.

THE REALITY OF THIS RECESSION

On Thursday, September 15, 2008, the U.S. economy had a heart attack.

The first symptoms occurred at 1 a.m. ET when Lehman Brothers, a storied investment bank dating back to 1844, announced it would file for Chapter 11 bankruptcy. By 11 a.m., one hour after the opening of the New York Stock Exchange, the Federal Reserve noticed a draw-down of $550 billion from money market accounts.

The fed delivered emergency CPR, backing up the money markets with $150 billion. It was too little, too late to prevent an electronic run on the major banks. So the fed took emergency action and closed down electronic withdrawals from banks and money markets. If they hadn't, investors were on pace to withdraw $5.5 trillion by 2 p.m., collapsing the entire U.S. economy by the end of the day, soon to be followed 24 hours later by the world economy.

That's the reason the then-Secretary of the Treasury, Henry Paulson, asked Congress to approve $700 billion of TARP funds to prop up teetering banks and stabilize the economy. It worked. The U.S. economy is still in the hospital, but seems to be recovering.

THE DOCTOR WILL SEE YOU NOW

Think of this book as a doctor's diagnosis followed by a recovery plan that will empower you to live a long, prosperous life. In the first two chapters, I'll be like a cardiologist who gives a real diagnosis of what caused the economic heart attack. Some of those causes were lifestyle choices: Wall Street was over-greedy. Bankers were over-leveraged. Consumers were over-spending. And businesses were over-expanding.

Yes, the patient brought this crisis on himself, but in a medical emergency (or an economic emergency) the top priority is to save the patient's life. We'll worry about lifestyle changes down the road. As you will learn in the coming pages, there's plenty of blame to go around. I spend Section 1 of this book analyzing the factors that contributed to our economic heart attack and the reason it will take years, not just months, for the economy to recover.

I'm not being negative.

I'm just being real.

Keep that in mind as you read the opening chapters.

WE'LL BOUNCE BACK

Also keep in mind that America is resilient. As Warren Buffett remarked, we've been through much worse as a country and survived. We've survived a revolution. A civil war. A near-bankruptcy of the Federal Reserve Bank. A Great Depression. A dozen recessions. Two world wars. And a terrorist attack on the World Trade Center. We not only survived those challenges, but we came back from them stronger than ever.

September 15, 2008, was a wakeup call.

The economy is still in intensive care, but the patient is responding to treatment.

Now it's time to talk about making changes that will make us stronger.

That's what Section 2 and Section 3 are about—think of these chapters as a personal recovery program that will explain how you, along with thousands of other Americans, can survive this recession and come back stronger than ever.

Just like we've always done in the past.

Dedication

*To those who have the vision and the courage to
choose entrepreneurship over entitlements*

Acknowledgment

A large and long-overdue thanks go to the graphic artists who have designed and laid out my books and publications for more than a decade, Jack and Elizabeth Parry of Parry Design Studio, Inc.

You two do great work.

But more importantly, you're great people.

I'd tell you I was looking forward to working with you for another couple of decades, but the thought of your having to put up with my obsessive-compulsive nature for 20 or more years would likely send you screaming into the night.

So, I'll just settle for this public proclamation: Jack and Elizabeth Parry, you bring out the best in my books while negotiating around the worst in my nature.

I thank you for your rare talents.

And applaud you for your even temperaments.

Okay, enough of the mushy stuff. Now get back to work!

Books by Dr. Steve Price

- *Dream Making in a Dream-Taking World*
- *Household Gold*
- *WWW. Stands for "World Wide Whiners"*

Contents

Introduction: The Perfect Recession 1

SECTION 1: THE PROBLEM

1 The Dirty Dozen: The 12 Key Causes
of the Perfect Recession. 15
2 From Recession to Resetting. 41

SECTION 2: THE PROMISES

3 Entitlements Become Expectations. 53
4 Releasing Your Inner Entrepreneur. 63

SECTION 3: THE SOLUTION

5 The Return to the "Real" American Dream 75
6 Pyramid Schemes:
Capitalists without a Conscience. 83
7 Altruistic Marketing™:
Capitalism with a Conscience 95

Conclusion: Your Moment on the Bridge 109

Introduction:
The Perfect Recession

Like the Perfect Storm, the Perfect Recession is a combination of regularly occurring circumstances that, taken singly, could have been easily absorbed into the global economy.

But when numerous negative economic factors came together at the same time, we got slammed by the Perfect Recession, a once-in-100-years phenomenon.

Introduction

The Perfect Recession

Current recession worst in 100 years.
—headline in the *Financial Times*

The Perfect Storm, they called it.

On Halloween, 1991, an unnamed monster storm 2,000 miles wide and stretching from Jamaica to Nova Scotia, churned across the North Atlantic and smashed into the northeastern coast of North America.

Packing winds over 100 miles per hour and whipping up waves as high as 100 feet, the storm washed away hundreds of waterfront homes. This Frankenstein of storms was later chronicled in Sebastian Junger's book, *The Perfect Storm*, which became the basis of a blockbuster movie of the same name.

What events transformed a flagging, late-season storm heading harmlessly away from the coast into a Goliath, once-in-100-years Perfect Storm that caused half a billion dollars of damage up and down the Eastern Seaboard and killed 12 people, including all six crew members onboard the *Andrea Gail* fishing boat?

"It was an unprecedented set of separate circumstances, each of which could have created a strong storm," explained meteorologist Bob Case, who tracked the storm and coined the term "the Perfect Storm". "But with all these contributing factors coming together at the right time, it was like throwing gasoline onto a raging fire."

The Perfect Storm started out as Hurricane Grace, a fizzled out, Level 2 hurricane about to be swallowed up by the vast open waters of the Atlantic Ocean. Then the unpredictable happened—a massive cold front from Canada collided with the hurricane's wet, warm air, creating violent updrafts and swirling winds that rejuvenated the moribund storm and wrenching its path 180 degrees back toward the U.S. coastline. With the warm currents of the Gulf Stream acting like a fuel injector on a Formula One racecar, the winds accelerated, pushing giant waves toward the shoreline. The storm crashed into the coastline just as a record high tide was cresting, adding another seven feet to the 30-foot storm surge.

Separately, each of the five contributors to the Perfect Storm would have had little impact on people and property: Normally, Hurricane Grace would have run out of gas... the Gulf Stream would have continued its lazy, northbound Atlantic journey... the low-pressure area and cold front from Canada would have dissolved in the warm October days... and the high tide would have spilled harmlessly over low-lying seawalls before making its regular retreat.

But when these normally unspectacular meteorological effects came together at just the right time under just the right circumstances, the result was a rare storm of terrifying proportions. A Perfect Storm.

THE MAKINGS OF THE PERFECT RECESSION

As I write this, we're in the midst of what I call "the Perfect Recession," which began in December of 2007. Like the Perfect Storm, the Perfect Recession is a combination of regularly occurring economic circumstances that, taken singly, could have been painlessly absorbed into the global economy, much as the Atlantic Ocean sops up dozens of tropical depressions during the summer months. But when numerous negative economic circumstances came together at the same time, we got slammed by a Perfect Recession, which cuts deeper and lasts longer than run-of-the-mill recessions.

Unlike the Perfect Storm, which had five major contributing factors, the Perfect Recession is even more complex, with more than a dozen events and circumstances contributing to the ongoing economic meltdown. And unlike a tropical storm, which lasts days, recessions last months—and can even last years—as is the case with Japan, which lingered in a growth-smothering recession for more than a decade.

WHAT'S THE DIFFERENCE BETWEEN A RECESSION AND A DEPRESSION?

There's an old joke about the difference between a recession and a depression: If your neighbor loses his job, it's a recession. If you lose your job, it's a depression.

The more commonly accepted definition is that a *recession* occurs when the gross domestic product (GDP is defined as the market value of all the goods and services made within the borders of a country in a year) declines for two consecutive quarters. A *depression* is a deep, prolonged recession. The U.S. has had multiple recessions since the end of WWII but only one depression in the 20th century—the Great Depression from 1929 to 1942.

Recessions aren't anything out of the ordinary. They're just part of the boom-and-bust business cycle, occurring every four or five years. The current recession, which began in the fall of 2007, is the 10th since the end of WWII. Recessions typically last 10 to 12 months. Here are the previous recessions and their lengths:

LENGTH OF RECESSIONS SINCE WWII

1948–49:	11 months
1953–54:	10 months
1957–58:	8 months
1960–61:	10 months
1969–70:	11 months
1973–75:	16 months
1980–82:	22 months
1990–91:	8 months
2001:	8 months
2007:	? months (or years?)

As this chart makes clear, recessions typically come and go, lasting anywhere from 8 to 22 months. If history is any indicator, by the end of '09, we should be out of this recession and well on our way to four or five boom years as we move into the second decade of the 21st century.

Not so fast.

The recession of '07 isn't your run-of-the-mill recession—it's more of a run-for-the hills recession—the Perfect Recession, if you will. The Great Depression lasted 13 years from start to finish, reminding us that down cycles can hang around for a decade or more. Just look to Japan, whose 1990 recession lasted 15 years, and today, nearly 20 years after the Nikkei stock index collapsed, Japanese housing prices have climbed back to only 40% of their 1990 values.

How long the Perfect Recession will last is anyone's guess. But just because the economy *technically* shows a return to growth doesn't mean we should break into a chorus of *Happy Days Are Here Again.* We only wish the situation were that rosy. Many economists are predicting a "jobless recovery," meaning the economy will grow, but unemployment will remain near

10% for years to come. (Add the underemployed... people seeking full-time work but settling for part-time employment... people being forced to accept early retirement... and people who have given up looking for work, the unemployment figure is closer to 20%).

Larry Summers, top economic advisor to the president, is less than optimistic about the speed of an economic recovery: "The economy is not going back to normal for quite some time. Our problems weren't made in a month or a year, and they won't be fixed in a month or a year."

Summers is right. As you will discover in this book, our economy is a tangled ball of yarn made of political miscues, misplaced values, corporate malfeasance, and monstrous personal, private, and public debt that will take years to unwind.

HOW WE COULD HAVE AVOIDED THIS MESS

I grew up hearing stories about the Great Depression.

My dad was a teenager when the stock market crashed in 1929. Mom was only nine. For the next 13 years, they and their families, with four children in my mom's family and five in my dad's, lived hand to mouth.

Born and raised in Duggar, Indiana, a one-street, no-stoplight coal-mining town carved into the thickly wooded hills in southern Indiana, my parents started dating when my mom was 19 and married a year later. Sure, they dreamed of a better life, but they were too worried where their next meal would come from to entertain grandiose thoughts of someday living the American Dream.

Opportunity? Wasn't any in Duggar. In the heart of the depression, unemployment across the country was 25%, but when the coal miners in Duggar were on strike, which was most of the time, unemployment in the 1930s was 90%. My dad never had a full-time job until age 28, when he joined the Army Air Corps. My mother owned two dresses during her four years in high school. She'd wash one and wear the other, alternating every other day for four years.

Those were the stories I grew up hearing.

If everyone in the United States grew up hearing those stories, I doubt our economy would be in this mess. Both businesspeople and consumers would be tighter fisted and more conservative with their investments. There would have been fewer subprime and "liar loans" approved. Fewer gambles taken by bankers who should have known better. Fewer credit cards issued. Fewer home equity loans green lighted. Fewer bad bank loans. Fewer foreclosures. Fewer bankruptcies. Fewer people buying houses they really couldn't afford. And fewer votes in Congress supporting legislation that will add trillions more to our federal debt.

But most Americans were born during a time when parents told their children very different stories from the ones I heard. Instead of hearing cautionary tales, kids heard stories about receiving a new car as a 16th birthday present. Stories about the "need" for $500 designer handbags. Stories about 10-day cruises and weeklong ski vacations. Stories about buying now with credit cards, and paying later with home equity loans. Stories that the stock market always goes up and up and up. Stories about letting the good times roll on and on.

So, consumers... and the federal government... and states... and municipalities... and even retirees on fixed incomes... spent and spent and spent, while banks and insurance companies, which were supposed to be rational, no-risk, conservative guardians of capital, gambled with stock-holder money like a drunk, trust-fund teenager on a casino boat.

Until one day, beginning in September of 2008, just 16 years after the Perfect Storm sank the 70-foot fishing boat, the *Andrea Gail*, the Perfect Recession is sinking our economy. Glug. Glug. Glug.

Now what do we do?

PURPOSE OF THIS BOOK

I have three main purposes in writing this book. One, I want to explain in easy-to-understand language how we got into this mess and who's to blame for it; two, I want you to understand why this Perfect Recession threatens to erode our prosperity and last for years; and three, I want you to learn how you and your family can not only survive the Perfect Recession, but thrive in the years ahead.

Let me start by telling you what this book is *not*.

This book is *not* an economics textbook that only Pulitzer Prize-winning economists can understand. Anyone who can read a cereal box will be able to read and understand this book.

This book is *not* a right-wing attack on left-leaning politicians. There is plenty of blame to spread around to politicians from both parties who are more interested in lining their own pockets than in protecting the American people.

This book is *not* an **oversimplification** of the causes of the Perfect Recession. Yes, I will **simplify** the contributing factors so that anyone can understand them. But *I will not oversimplify a complex problem* by blaming the whole thing on the Democrats' support for subprime mortgages. Yes, allowing low-income people with lousy credit to get mortgages with no money down was a harebrained idea that played a part in the economic meltdown. But, as you will learn in Chapter 1, subprime mortgages are just *one* of more than a *dozen factors* that contributed to the Perfect Storm.

I SEEK INFORMATION, NOT JUST CONFIRMATION

There's a lot of talk these days about bias in the mass media.

That's why I gather information from both sides of the political spectrum. I read my hometown newspaper, the *Tampa Tribune*, each morning. But I also read *The Wall Street Journal* in the afternoon. I read *Time* and *Newsweek*, but I also read the *National Review*, first published in 1955 by William F. Buckley, founder of the modern-day conservative movement.

My point is this: In researching and writing this book, I did my best to gather information from as many sources as possible. In doing so, I came to this conclusion: There's plenty of blame to spread around, starting with politicians from both parties who sold their votes in Congress for campaign contributions from special interest groups. More about them in the next chapter.

CONNECT THE DOTS

There's no shortage of information about this recession in the media and the blogosphere. We're drowning in a sea of facts and figures and opinions. But what is missing is a cohesive theory that connects the dots and draws a pattern that makes sense of all these bits and bites of information.

That's why I wrote this book—to connect the dots and draw you a picture of a ship being tossed like the *Andrea Gail* in the Perfect Storm. Except in this picture, the ocean is the global economy, the storm is the Perfect Recession, and the ship is your personal household—your family... your home... your career... your nest egg... your retirement savings... your future... and your version of the American Dream.

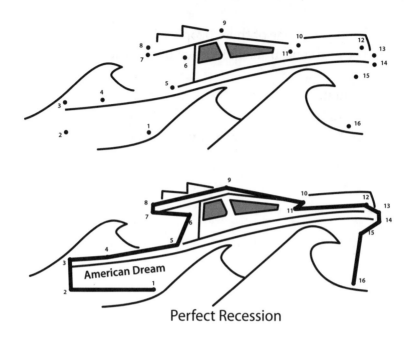

Perfect Recession

In the coming pages, I'm going to explain in simple terms what created this economic Perfect Storm and how you can navigate your ship to a safe harbor while the Perfect Recession is raging and ravaging millions of households around the globe.

When seasoned sailors see a storm approaching, they stay in harbor until calmer seas prevail. But occasionally storms seem to come out of nowhere, gathering and strengthening too quickly for sailors to heed. The Perfect Storm was one of those.

So, too, the Perfect Recession.

Most people, including Wall Street bankers and billion-dollar investors, were caught unprepared as the Perfect Recession smashed into the economy. Prepared or not, the Perfect Recession is here, and we have to deal with it.

So, if you're one of those people who didn't make it to the safe port of financial independence before the storm hit, this book is for you.

Read it.

Act on the advice.

And prosper in the stormy years ahead.

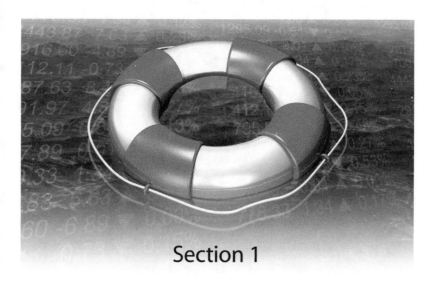

Section 1

The Problem

*I don't make this stuff up.
I just report what I read
in the newspapers.*

—Will Rogers,
American humorist

Chapter 1

The Dirty Dozen: The 12 Key Causes of the Perfect Recession

Political pundits on both sides of the political aisle oversimplify things, reducing complex issues to simple soundbites and slogans so they can assign blame to the opposing party.

In the case of the Perfect Recession, it's not that simple. The Perfect Recession was caused by 12 key factors that transformed what would normally be a run-of-the-mill recession into a run-for-the-hills economic tsunami that will take years to recover from.

Chapter 1

The Dirty Dozen: The 12 Key Causes of the Perfect Recession

> *This is the most troubling economy and the worst bear market I've ever seen. Our system has failed.*
> —Jack Bogle,
> 80-year-old founder of
> Vanguard Funds

In his classic science-fiction novel *Fahrenheit 451*, Ray Bradbury describes a future where a fireman's job is, ironically, to burn books. The book's title comes from the temperature at which paper bursts into flames—451 degrees Fahrenheit.

The fire chief, Capt. Beatty, explains that books are burned because they complicate people's lives by challenging them to think. The ruling authorities reason that when people are released from the demands of thinking, it makes their lives simpler and easier—making them easier to control, of course:

"What traitors books can be," complains Capt. Beatty. *"You think they're backing you up, and then they turn on you. Other people can use them, too, and there you are, lost in the middle of*

the moor, in a great welter of nouns and verbs and adjectives." The ultimate beauty of fire, argues the fire chief, is that it "destroys responsibility and consequences." Which is why the ruling authorities replace books with a steady diet of easy-to-repeat-and-understand slogans and sound bites.

THE FULL FACTS ABOUT THE CAUSES OF THE PERFECT RECESSION

As in *Fahrenheit 451*, today there are political pundits in positions of power and influence who want you to think in sound bites and slogans so you can point fingers and place blame on one political party or one social program.

Fact is, it's not that simple.

"Facts are stubborn things," Ronald Reagan often said. Yes, they are. Especially when they fly in the face of our beliefs. But as Abraham Lincoln said, "Ignoring the facts doesn't make them less true." (Nor does trumpeting key facts that fit an agenda while conveniently ignoring the facts that don't, a skill at which so many "spin doctors" in the media excel.)

So, let's enter the "no-spin zone," to use Bill O'Reilly's opening tagline, and get ready to learn the facts and full truth about the 12 factors that created the Perfect Recession. Certainly some factors leading up to the Perfect Recession have had a bigger impact than others. But by and large, we would be in a run-of-the-mill recession with a small "r" instead of a Perfect Recession if so many key factors hadn't coalesced at the same time.

Here's my list of the Dirty Dozen contributors to the once-in-100-years recession:

16

DIRTY DOZEN CAUSES OF THE PERFECT RECESSION
1) Securitization
2) Subprime loan crisis
3) Financial institutions deemed "too big to fail"
4) Financial derivatives
5) Housing bubble
6) Commercial real estate bubble
7) Politicians wanting to stay in office
8) Deregulation
9) Globalization
10) Consumer culture
11) Rating agencies
12) Fed Chairman Alan Greenspan

Let's spend the rest of this chapter talking about each of these major contributors to the global economic crisis, starting with "securitization," financial instruments originated by the wizards of Wall Street to make them richer than even they ever imagined.

1) SECURITIZATION

Since the founding of the New York Stock Exchange in 1887 under a buttonwood tree in lower Manhattan, tradable investments, called "securities," have come in two basic flavors—*stocks*, which enable investors to buy ownership in public companies; or *bonds*, which allow people to profit by loaning money to companies and/or the government.

Then, in the early 1970s, Lewis Ranieri, a Wall Street bond trader, got the bright idea to have private lenders, such as mortgage bankers and savings and loans, in cooperation with the three giant government-sponsored housing guarantors—Fannie Mae, Freddie Mac, and Ginnie Mae, which own about 50% of the home mortgages in this country—to securitize pools of mortgages into mortgage-backed securities (MBS) and sell them to investors. At the time, this seemed like a great deal for everybody. Investors in MBS got some of the highest yields of any government security, and the MBS allowed banks to transfer risk to investors because the bank was no longer obliged to hold mortgages, allowing bankers to originate more loans (which was good for homeowners) and make more money (which was good for the banks). Securitization of mortgages was so successful that it was quickly applied to any asset class with a cashflow, including car loans, student loans, and credit card debt.

So far, so good.

But there was a nasty unintended consequence of securitization that busy bankers, drunk on their profits, failed to foresee: When the economy slowed, the flow of cash that securitization depended on started to flow less freely, like a crimped garden hose. The first crimp in the securitized pipeline started when thousands of low-income homeowners holding subprime mortgages stopped making their monthly mortgage payments. Subprime defaults quickly spread to other mortgage holders who bought at the top of the housing bubble, resulting in monthly mortgage payments they couldn't afford. Foreclosure signs and for sale signs flooded neighborhoods, causing housing prices to drift downward.

As the domino of subprime loans tilted and then tumbled, it bumped into other securitized debt—credit card holders started missing monthly minimum payments... car loans and leases started going unpaid... and student loans went into default. Within months, the bottom dropped out of the asset-backed securities business, and banks, insurance companies, pension funds, investors, and even governments (Iceland's government was forced to declare bankruptcy, while others are on the brink) were stuck with trillions of dollars in asset-based bonds that no one wanted to buy because they were losing value with no end in sight.

2) SUBPRIME LOAN CRISIS

Securitization and the subprime meltdown go together like a horse and carriage—you can't have one without the other. Securitization became a huge contributor to the Perfect Recession because it changed the dynamic of mortgage lending. Here's why:

Before securitization, banks held many mortgages in their portfolios, so they lent only to credit-worthy borrowers. But once securitization came into play, banks realized that instead of making small profits by holding mortgages for years, they could make big profits in less than a month by originating loans and then quickly selling them to the government or to giant mortgage companies, such as Countrywide. Banks thought, "H-m-m-m, if I can get my money upfront, and if it's not my problem if mortgage holders can't make their monthly payments, why be so picky about who qualifies for a loan?"

As a result, lending standards went from strict (20% down, high credit score, and two years of salary history) to non-existent (0% down, no documentation of income or payment histories), opening the door for people with low incomes and lousy credit to "buy" houses with subprime mortgages. In 2005, virtually anybody with a pulse could qualify for a no-documentation "Liar Loan," which is why we see stories on TV about lawn service workers earning less than $25,000 a year getting mortgages to buy $750,000 homes.

Although subprime loans comprise only 7% of the total global crisis, like a snowball growing larger as it rolls down the mountain, defaults on subprime loans triggered the economic avalanche that become the Perfect Recession.

The challenge with the subprime meltdown isn't the size of losses—*The Wall Street Journal* estimates that defaults on subprime loans make up no more than $1 trillion of the loss of $50 trillion in stocks, commodities, real estate, business loans, and hard-to-trace derivatives. The biggest challenge facing banks and investors is determining the value of the mortgage-backed securities and other complex derivatives they own. Who in his right mind will buy an asset if no one knows the value?

For instance, a $300,000 subprime mortgage in Charlotte, North Carolina, is likely worth 90% of its value, whereas that same $300,000 mortgage in over-built Las Vegas may be valued at 40%, meaning when the bank owning the mortgage sells, it will book a loss of $180,000.

Banks are understandably hesitating to accept losses that large, which is why trillions of dollars in "toxic assets" are frozen. So the economy remains stuck in neutral. And if that's not bad enough, banks are sitting on trillions of dollars of commercial loans for malls, shopping centers, and office buildings that will soon go into default (more about that later).

And who holds the lion's share of troubled commercial loans and other wobbly assets? The mega-banks deemed "too big to fail," led by Citibank... Bank of America... JP Morgan Chase... and Wells Fargo. What does "too big to fail" mean, and how does that contribute to the Perfect Recession?

Keep reading to find out.

3) FINANCIAL INSTITUTIONS "TOO BIG TO FAIL"

According to *Fortune* magazine, the big four banks hold half of U.S. credit card and business loans and "account for most of the problem securities that haunt the industry." Most economists and financial leaders agree that letting one or more of these banks fail would throw the global economy into a tailspin, leading to more bankruptcies and frozen lending.

The $700 billion from the U.S. government to bail out big banks raised lots of good questions from outraged taxpayers: Why reward bad banking policies by bailing them out? Isn't that "privatizing profits and socializing losses"? Isn't that un-American, and, well, just plain unfair? Why is the government giving $700 billion of taxpayer money to bail out greedy Wall Street billionaires? Where's the bailout for Main Street? Why give millions in bonuses to AIG employees who are on the hook for $180 billion in taxpayer money while millions of honest, middle-class people are losing their jobs and losing their homes?

To understand what "too big to fail" means, let's use an analogy: Think of the worldwide free market economy as a living, breathing human. In this analogy, the international banking community, dominated by the U.S., is the heart of the free market system. The mega-banks and giant financial institutions, like Citigroup and AIG Insurance and 20 to 30 others, are the chambers and valves that make the heart function properly. Capital—in the form of cash, loans, and credit—is the blood. Big businesses are the organs; free enterprise is the arteries and veins the capital flows through; and we ordinary citizens, you and I and everyone other person in the world, are the cells.

In September of 2008, the world economy had a heart attack. The banking system stopped pumping. The U.S.

government played emergency room doctor and pulled out a $700 billion defibrillator and shocked the heart, restoring the heartbeat and stabilizing the patient while surgeons figure out the best method of treatment to restore the long-term health of the patient. If the heart dies, the blood supply to the organs and cells is cut off, which means when the capital from banks stops flowing, there's no credit... no business loans... no car loans... airlines stop flying... manufacturers stop making things... people stop buying—and then consumers, you and I and everyone on Main Street, are cut off from capital, and we die a slow death.

Some people make the argument that years of self-abuse led to this heart attack, and that poorly managed banks deserve to go out of business, which is certainly true. But here's the harsh reality: The failure of a mega-bank poses what economists call *systemic risks*, which means their failure can threaten the life of the entire banking system.

If Wall Street fails, it takes Main Street down with it, pure and simple.

Take the case of AIG, an insurance company the government has deemed too big to fail. Why give $180 billion in bailout money to just one company—an insurance company, at that? Because AIG owns hundreds of thousands of complex, insurance-type contracts on investments and financial instruments owned by thousands of banks worldwide. If AIG fails, it would be like pulling two or three cards from the bottom of a house of cards—the whole thing will tumble.

Is the concept of too big to fail wise? No. Is this fair? No. Is it good for the world economy? No. Is it good for America? No. Is it good for you and your family? No. But right now, this is the reality we have to live with until changes are made to the system.

4) FINANCIAL DERIVATIVES

In finance, a derivative is any financial instrument that "derives" its value from an already existing financial product. Car insurance, for example, is a type of derivative, and until recently, only insurance companies could create insurance-type derivative products.

Then in December of 2000, pressured by the banking lobbyists, the Senate passed the Commodity Futures Modernization Act, allowing banks and brokerages to create insurance-type products. In 2000, banks and other financial institutions introduced insurance-like products called "credit default swaps," or "swaps" for short. Swaps were essentially private insurance contracts that paid off when an investment went bad. But because swaps were unregulated, nobody had to actually own anything to insure it, which meant, in effect, that traders working for banks and insurance companies could place bets on everything from interest rates to currency exchanges to, of course, mortgages, even the ones they didn't own.

Like Vegas, the riskier the bet, the bigger the return, and among mortgages, subprime loans were the riskiest. As long as the holders of subprime loans made their monthly payments, the banks raked in the loot. Bankers reasoned they were on the safe side of the bet because mortgages seldom go into default—even the subprime ones.

Oops—beginning in 2007, "seldom" happened. Holders of subprime loans started defaulting in droves. In a 16-month period, 30% of subprime loans went into default; eventually, that figure hit 60%. Just as you would call your insurance company and ask for compensation if your house burned down, holders of swaps called the banks and asked to be paid for their losses. The big difference is that with swaps, you weren't limited to insuring just your home. With swaps, you could insure your neighbor's house. Or the neighborhood. Or the whole city, for that matter. Pay your premiums, get your swaps. And investors who bet against subprime loans raked in the dough.

Insurance premiums, as you well know, cost only a fraction of the value of the item being insured, so the payout can be 20... 30... 50... even 100 times the premiums. One hedge fund manager who predicted the housing bubble invested $10 million in swaps, betting against subprime loans. He pocketed $3.7 billion in less than a year.

Big problem for the financial institutions who were acting as insurers—there wasn't enough money behind their commitments. To a large extent, that's what led to the demise of Bear Sterns and Lehman Brothers and put AIG on government life support. They made bigger bets than they could pay off, and when the insured parties knocked on their doors to collect, the money wasn't there.

Warren Buffett called derivatives "financial weapons of mass destruction" for a very good reason: Because derivatives are largely unregulated, nobody knows how much capital backed by derivatives is floating around the global banking system. Experts peg the derivative market at anywhere between $30 trillion on the low side... to $500 trillion on the high side.

The storm clouds just keep building.

5) HOUSING BUBBLE

One every 13 seconds—that's how fast foreclosures were racking up in 2009. As I write this, 30% of all mortgaged property is "underwater," meaning the home, due to falling prices, is worth less than the mortgage amount. In the first quarter of 2009, a record 20 million homes stood unoccupied, blighting neighborhoods and forcing homeowner associations to raise monthly rates on members who are paying their mortgages. The air is still leaking out of the housing balloon as prices continue to fall in most parts of the nation.

Who is to blame for the housing bubble? (We'll get to the bursting of the commercial real estate bubble later—that's a whole other bucket of writhing eels.) Certainly much of the blame belongs to Barney Frank and his cohorts in Congress who resisted reforming Fannie Mae and Freddie Mac, the two Government Sponsored Enterprises that laid the groundwork for the crisis.

Fannie and Freddie buy mortgages from lenders, such as savings and loans and banks, and then pool them and securitize them, selling the resulting bonds to investors. But as the Democrats insisted that lenders make more mortgages available to low-income earners, loose lending standards got jokingly lax, and the subprime debacle started its short ride over a high cliff.

But it's naïve to say that Barney Frank is solely responsible for the housing crisis. There was plenty of blame to spread around, including the Federal Reserve, led by Alan Greenspan, for keeping interest rates too low for too long, which further encouraged buyers to purchase homes in a bid-up market. According to *The Wall Street Journal*, "Mortgage loan originations increased an average of 56% per year for three years—from $1.05 trillion in 2000 to $3.95 trillion in 2003."

At the height of the bubble, the median price for a home was $231,000, which pushed monthly housing expenses (mortgage principle and interest, property taxes, insurance, and private mortgage insurance) to more than $2,000 per month, 50% or more of the average American family's monthly take-home pay.

In 1978, the average home price was 2.5 times household income, which means a couple making $50,000 could afford a $125,000 home; 2006 prices reached nearly *five times family income*, spiking the average home price to nearly $250,000. Lenders not only went along with the increased ratio, they were asking zero percent down and no financial documentation. In short, for housing prices to hit bottom, they need to fall 40% to 50% from the highs of 2006, bottoming out somewhere between $115,000 to $140,000. In over-built areas of the country, such as Las Vegas, Florida, and California, abandoned properties have dropped 60% and 70%.

Residential real estate has tanked, big time, but right behind it an even bigger shoe is about to drop—commercial real estate.

6) COMMERCIAL REAL ESTATE BUBBLE

In the spring of 2009, General Properties, the second-biggest shopping mall owner, with 200 regional shopping centers in 44 states, filed for Chapter 11 bankruptcy—the largest real estate bankruptcy in history.

Mark my words—there will be many more to follow.

"Commercial landlords continue to lose retail tenants at an accelerating pace," writes *The Wall Street Journal*, "indicating that the industry's troubles are worsening." As the Perfect Recession lengthens, companies struggling to reduce costs dumped 25 million square feet of office space in one quarter, hurtling the vacancy rate toward 20% and forcing property owners to lower their rents to attract tenants. Vacancies and lower rents mean less revenue, causing the value of buildings to plummet, often below the amount of their mortgages.

The woes of commercial real estate pose a huge threat to the economy because of the sheer size of the debt—$3.5

trillion, which is more than the combined debt of auto loans, credit cards, and student loans. To complicate matters, $700 billion of commercial mortgages were sliced up, securitized, and sold to big investors, such as state and municipal pension funds, non-profit foundations, and college endowments.

And guess who holds most of the nearly $3 trillion in loans to this shaky sector? That would be banks and insurance companies deemed "too big to fail." But because many regional banks too small to receive government bailout money are holding big loans on buildings, hotels, stores, and malls, they're destined to go under when big borrowers default on their loans. *The Wall Street Journal* estimates that 3,000 small to mid-size banks suffer from over-exposure to wobbly commercial real estate loans, and one west coast research firm anticipates 700 to 1,000 mid-sized banks could fail as a result of their exposure to commercial real estate.

The looming crisis in commercial real estate can be summed up as too much space chasing too few customers compounded by too much debt. To complicate matters, once General Properties comes out of bankruptcy with reduced debt, they'll be able to slash rates and draw tenants from other malls, creating a downward spiral that will force competitors to follow suit and file for bankruptcy.

"We're only at the beginning of a hurricane that may continue for at least the next 18 to 24 months," said Victor Calanog, a research director for Reis, Inc., a New York-based research company specializing in commercial property. Sale prices of even the most prestigious buildings in the country are dropping like a stone in a vacuum. The marquee John Hancock Tower in Boston that sold for $1.3 billion in 2006 sold in a foreclosure auction less than three years later for $660.6 million, a 50% discount.

If the John Hancock Tower, a marquee AA property in a great location in one of the healthiest cities in the U.S. sells for half price, what does that portend for the rest of the market? Well, when the last taxpayer is finally flat broke and penniless from bailing out all the banks too big to fail, we can always sleep on those cushy couches in the malls and office lobbies.

Why not? We'll own them—along with GM, Chrysler, AIG, and who knows what else as the Perfect Recession roars on and on....

7) POLITICIANS WANTING TO STAY IN OFFICE

"Democracy is the worst system of government in the world," quipped Winston Churchill, "except for all the others." Although superior to any other governing system, democracy has inherent flaws, and two of the biggest flaws— lobbyists and campaign contributions—have been getting more pronounced with each passing year.

Let's look at lobbyists first. The goal of a lobbyist is to get the ear of a congressperson in order to get legislation passed (or rescinded) that will benefit the lobbyist's cause or company. Fair enough. But in recent years, the ranks of lobbyists have been filled by ex-senators and representatives who have personal relationships with our elected officials and an inner knowledge of how the legislative process works. It makes for an unfair advantage to the firms the lobbyists represent.

Little wonder, then, that the top lobbying effort during the last decade was led by mega-banks, which spent $383 million on lobbying for laws to deregulate banking, which then led to the derivatives disaster and the "banks-too-big-to-fail" phenomenon. The next two biggest lobbying industries were insurance companies, led by none other than AIG, followed by investment securities firms, which dropped $60 million a year during the last 10 years trying to push their agenda through Congress.

The two biggest culprits in the subprime mess, Fannie Mae and Freddie Mac, spent $170 million in 10 years in their lobbying efforts, employing 91 ex-elected officials from both political parties, including House leaders Tom DeLay and Newt Gingrich. In 2006, Freddie Mac paid former House Speaker Gingrich $300,000 to help fight off potential regulation.

It used to be that retired politicians would go back to their home states after serving in Congress. Today, they remain in Washington, pulling down big checks from lobbying groups and enjoying their residual political power. It's bad ethics and bad for the country.

An even bigger threat to our economy than lobbyists is the current system of campaign contributions. It takes big bucks to get elected these days, which means that to get elected, politicians must auction off their political influence to the highest bidders. Two of the biggest campaign contributors from 1989 to 2008 were Fannie Mae and Freddie Mac, which contributed a total of $4.8 million to political candidates, with democrats receiving 57% of that.

Of the top recipients of Fannie and Freddie campaign money, five were Democrats and five were Republicans. The investment made big returns for the people at the top of Fannie and Freddie. Twenty of Fannie's top executives—including three lobbyists—earned $1 million each in 2002, with nine managers dividing up more than $3 million. The CEO of Fannie, Frank Raines, received $90 million in total compensation from 1998 to 2003.

The Wall Street Journal reported that AIG, which is into U.S. taxpayers for $180 billion so far, contributed generously to the political campaigns of key figures in both parties. Since 1989, Chris Dodd has received $281,000 from AIG. No big surprise there. But second on the list is George W. Bush, who received more than $200,000, followed by John McCain, who received nearly $100,000.

Were the contributions illegal? No. Were they unethical? You decide.

All I know is if you want to know which politicians contributed the most to the Perfect Recession, just follow the money.

8) DEREGULATION

Deregulation is like a pendulum—when it swings too far in the direction of over-regulation, it restricts free markets and chokes profits; when it swings too far in favor of laissez faire capitalism, it encourages excesses—such as AIG gambling, and losing, $180 billion on credit default swaps—and invites unsustainable bubbles, as was the case with the tech bubble that burst in 2002 and the housing bubble that popped in 2006.

For the past 25 years, the pendulum of deregulation has swung too far in favor of the banks and insurance companies. It's time to push the pendulum back to the middle.

When markets are poorly regulated for too long a period, unethical capitalists will step into the breech to make as much money as they can, anyway they can. A case in point of the downside of deregulation was the repeal of the Glass-Steagall Act, which was passed in the Great Depression to stabilize the banking system by prohibiting the merger of commercial banks and investment banks; further deregulation legalized "off-balance sheet accounting," which enabled banks to hide liabilities and participate in high-risk investments, such as credit default swaps and crazy-complex derivatives. Lax enforcement of anti-monopoly laws encouraged big banks to acquire competitors, leading to mega-banks that are "too big to fail;" and also allowed banks to make obscene profits in the go-go years leading up to October of 2007, when the air started leaking out of the balloon.

Deregulation of credit cards permitted banks to charge interest in excess of 30% and to foist cards on financially inexperienced 18-year-old college students, knowing that their parents would take over the payments when the balance got too big for Timmy or Tammy to handle. Deregulation of Wall Street and a watered-down Securities and Exchange Commission enabled Bernie Madoff to operate the biggest Ponzi scheme in history, causing $65 billion in losses to 13,500 investors that included hospital foundations, charitable organizations, widows, pensioners, and, yes, even friends and relatives.

"Sensible regulations are in order," writes a professor of finance in *The Wall Street Journal*. "Most of us drive cars even though they sometimes crash. But we also insist that cars are made safe and that speed limits and other rules of the road are enforced." Rogue capitalists on Wall Street drove the global economy into a deep ditch, and once it's back on the road again, it's up to Washington to make sure they don't hand the keys to drunk brokers and bankers again.

9) GLOBALIZATION

In 2007 and 2008, when the stock market was in free fall, the "decoupling theory" was making the rounds of Wall Street investors. Decoupling believes that because many developing nations have growing economies, especially China, India, and Brazil, their markets will remain strong even when the U.S. tips into a recession.

Money managers who invested in foreign stocks in 2008 based on this theory found out the hard way the difference between theory and reality, as foreign markets plunged as deeply, if not deeper, than the U.S. stock exchanges, which lost 45% of its value in 2007-08. Although the U.S. is only 4% of the world population, our economy is still larger than the next four-biggest economies in the world combined, which is why the old adage "When America sneezes, the world catches pneumonia" still rings true.

Decoupling would make sense if the world's economies were connected like uncooked spaghetti in the box—each economy straight and rigid and separate. But in the global economy, national economies overlap and intertwine like cooked spaghetti on a plate—every strand touching every other strand, making national economies increasingly interdependent.

Because each nation has its own rules for regulating and financial transactions, when an international company declares bankruptcy, untangling the global web becomes nightmarish. When the 100-plus-year-old Lehman Brothers was forced to declare bankruptcy, for example, hundreds of banks and investment firms around the world sued to get back billions of invested in Lehman bonds and derivatives.

It will take years to untangle this knot. Here's why: A big part of Lehman's notes originated from the company's Amsterdam subsidiary, which operated mostly out of London, which means almost all the notes are governed by English law... while the validation of debt is under Dutch bankruptcy law... and obligations under the notes are governed by New York State law... while claims have to be calculated and filed in accordance with the bankruptcy laws of the United States.

What a nightmare!

And that's just the complications arising from one of 433 subsidiaries Lehman has around the globe—and there are 12 financial institutions with more subsidiaries than Lehman, topped by Citigroup, with 2,435 subsidiaries spread all over the world. Can you imagine what would happen if Citibank, the most underfunded mega-bank in the world, were allowed to fail? We could be facing a global depression that would make the Great Depression look like a bounced check.

10) CONSUMER CULTURE

Remember the parable of the ant and the grasshopper? The ant is disciplined, gathering food in the summer when the harvest is plenty and storing it for the lean winter months. The grasshopper "lives for today," eating and drinking everything in sight, partying as if the good times will never end. When winter arrives, the ant is prepared and survives. The grasshopper is doomed.

For the last 25 years, the typical U.S. consumer has been the grasshopper, spending too much today and saving too little for tomorrow. For a six-year period leading up to 2008, when the economy fire alarm sounded, signaling the party was over, the savings rate in the U.S. was −6%. Repeat, MINUS SIX PERCENT. (Compared to 1982, when the average household saved 11% of household income.) Consumers were supporting grasshopper lifestyles with ballooning credit card balances and home equity loans.

Then winter came in the form of the Perfect Recession.

Today, the average consumer is facing nearly $10,000 in credit card debt... pay decreases (if they still have a job)... little savings... depleted retirement accounts... with home equity declining daily (30% of homeowners owe more on their mortgages than their homes are worth).

How did we get in this mess? We got caught up in the Consumer Culture, buying into the myth that putting more stuff in bigger homes (the average home size increased by 50% in 25 years) would somehow make us happier. It only made us poorer. From 1980 to 2007, the median price of a new American home doubled. Not just in size, but in appointments. Countertops had to be granite, not Formica®. Appliances had to be gleaming stainless, not yucky white. Floors had to be hardwood, not carpeted. Televisions had to sit in entertainment centers, not on TV stands. Cars had to be new, not used (and preferably foreign, not domestic). Dinners had to be at restaurants, not home cooked. Family vacations had to be out of state, preferably cruises—with an upgraded stateroom, thank you very much.

Hey, all these perks are fine and dandy—if you have the cash to pay for them. But most consumers didn't. So, rather than deny themselves (or make more money to pay in cash), the Consumer Culture charged it. If that wasn't bad enough, our kids watched us throw around credit cards—and learned. Half of college students had run up more than $5,000 in credit card debt while in school, and a third had more than $10,000.

Then the Perfect Recession crashed into our cruise ship, flinging us overboard to tread water in an ocean of debt. Odd thing about consumer debt and big mortgages—sure is fun piling them up. But it's pure agony paying them off. If people knuckle down and start paying down those balances, it will take money out of our economy, further stalling a recovery. If people walk away from those obligations, it will trash their credit rating and stick banks—the ones who lend money to grow the economy—with more toxic assets, making them even more cautious to lend. Either way, consumers—who make up

70% of the U.S. economy—are tapped out, which will stifle economic growth for years to come.

11) RATING AGENCIES

The three major financial rating agencies—Moody's, Standard & Poors, and Fitch—are supposed to offer factual, non-biased ratings on thousands of stocks and bonds. And as long as investors were paying for the information, there was little incentive to fudge the numbers. By law, only securities rated by one or more of these agencies can be held in a money market or mutual fund account.

Indeed, up until a few years ago, investors could trust that "A"-rated bonds were safer and more secure than "B"- and "C"-rated bonds. Then the rating agencies, seeking more revenue, started allowing the bond issuers—who had a ton more money to spend than consumers—to pay for their ratings. Good deal for the agencies, bad deal for investors.

Now, think about this a second: The companies issuing the debt are now paying the salaries of the people rating that debt. Think a company might be a tad upset if they paid you $150,000 only to discover you rated their bond a "C" while slapping an "A" rating on a competitor's bond? Bond issuers started playing one agency against the other, demanding high ratings in exchange for their business. "If you won't give us an AAA rating," they'd threaten Moody's, "then we'll take our business to S&P or Fitch."

Not surprisingly, the big three rating agencies enjoyed their most profitable years ever during the decade leading up to the Perfect Recession. The conflict of interest got so out of whack that in early 2007, before the bottom fell out, the three rating agencies gave the highest rating to 37,000 structured financial products, including 60% of the products evaluated by Fitch. In 2006, 44% of Moody's revenues came from rating securitized products, such as mortgage-backed securities.

How corrupt were the agencies? All three rating agencies gave "A" ratings to Lehman Brothers bonds right until September 15, 2007, the day Lehman filed for bankruptcy. Little wonder, then, why the "big three" are facing a blizzard of lawsuits from pension plans and mutual funds that saw their "A" rated stocks and bonds drop 40% to 50% in 2008.

12) FED CHAIRMAN ALAN GREENSPAN

Federal Reserve Chairman Alan Greenspan, celebrated as the "maestro" for his ability to conduct the economy, headed up the Fed for 16 years, retiring in 2006. Unfortunately, maestro Greenspan conducted too loosely and stayed on the podium too long.

Almost three years after stepping down as chairman, a contrite Greenspan admitted he had discounted the need for financial regulations and put too much faith in the self-policing power of free markets. As far back as 1994, Greenspan staunchly and successfully opposed tighter regulation on derivatives. He also resisted calls for tighter regulation of subprime mortgages, and in 2004, he even endorsed adjustable rate mortgages (ARMs), arguing that their lower initial rate made them less expensive than fixed-rate mortgages and that consumers could always refinance when the rates adjusted upward. The Federal Reserve has the broad authority under the Home Owner Equity Protection Act, so Greenspan could have scaled back the housing boom by lowering the boom on loose lending. But instead, he waved his low interest rate wand and let the band play on.

That is, until, screech—rising housing prices put on the brakes in 2006 and started heading the other way. The maestro struck a sour note when he assumed that housing prices would always go up. He was wrong, and millions of upside-down mortgage holders are left holding a bag of bad advice.

I ask you, how are the nearly 30% of Americans who owe more on their mortgages than their houses are worth going to refinance to a lower rate? Answer: They aren't. And in two or three years, when the ARMs that were approved in 2006 at the height of the market adjust upward, we're going to see a whole new round of mortgage defaults and foreclosures.

More and more economists are blaming Greenspan for contributing greatly to the housing bubble (and the entire easy credit bubble, for that matter) by keeping interest rates too low for too long and for having too much faith in free markets to regulate themselves. Deregulation can lead to growth, but no regulation can lead to a crisis. And a crisis is what we are facing right now.

"I've found a flaw in my ideology," Greenspan told Congress. "I don't know how significant or permanent it is. But I've been very distressed by that fact."

"When asset bubbles build, the Fed should raise rates," writes Robert J. Barbera in *The Cost of Capitalism*. "The notion that the Fed should worry about systemic risk only after a crisis hits is madness." I have to agree that the word "madness" pretty well describes the events leading up to the Perfect Recession.

THE ECONOMIC GULF STREAM EFFECT

There you have it—the Dirty Dozen, the 12 key causes of the Perfect Recession. But unlike previous recessions that fizzled out in 12 to 18 months, this recession is destined to hang around for years into the future.

Why do I say that? Because just as the Gulf Stream of warm currents fed and intensified the Perfect Storm, a series

37

of economic changes and circumstances are feeding the Perfect Recession, ensuring that it will linger and continue on its destructive path far longer than most people anticipate, including the so-called "experts."

Let's turn to the next chapter to learn more about the economic "Gulf Stream factors" that will transform this Perfect Recession… into the Permanent Resetting.

Chapter 2

From Recession to Resetting

American consumers make up 70% of the U.S. economy, and for the past 25 years, they've been on a spending spree fueled by credit cards and rising equity in our homes.

The Perfect Recession put an end to that. The shop-'til-you-drop days are over, to be replaced by less spending, more saving, and higher taxes, which will slow down economic growth for years to come.

From Recession to Resetting

This downturn is different.
It will define a generation. We
didn't get into this overnight. And
we won't get out of it overnight.
—John G. Stumpf,
CEO of Wells Fargo Bank

The "New Normal."

You're going to hear that phrase a lot more in the coming months and years. The New Normal means that when the Perfect Recession finally ends (and the negative growth of the economy *will* end someday), we will not be returning to the spend-like-it'll-never-end '90s.

"The '90s are over, and we're never going back," says Roger McNamee, founder of a $2 billion private equity company, who coined the term and authored the book, *The New Normal.* "This downturn is fundamentally different," McNamee says. "Moving forward will be a resetting of the economic order."

We're in the process of moving from a *recession* to a *resetting*, which is unlike most previous post-recession years, when the U.S. economy grew by leaps and bounds following recessionary periods. This time, we'll still grow, but it will be by grunts and groans as credit becomes tighter, consumers save, and both the public and private sectors tighten their budgets and commit to paying back debt.

GULF STREAM EFFECT ON THE ECONOMY

Just as the Gulf Stream fed the Perfect Storm, there is an economic Gulf Stream feeding the Perfect Recession. These steady cultural currents and winds are changing our economic climate, but, unlike the Gulf Stream that warms Bermuda, the economic Gulf Stream will cool our economy for decades.

Keep in mind that American consumers make up 70% of the U.S. economy, and for the last 25 years, Americans have been on a shopping spree funded by credit cards and rising equity in our homes. We're not just in the midst of a major recession, we're at the forefront of a *major resetting*—a paradigm shift that will recalibrate America's economic growth... job prospects... household incomes... consumer attitudes... and spending. The shop-'til-you-drop days are over, to be replaced by less spending, more saving, and, unless we make a quick U-turn, more government entitlements that require more of your tax dollars to fund.

Here is a laundry list of the long-term forces that will put a long-lasting damper on our economy:

Social Security and Medicare: Baby boomers make up 25% of the U.S. population, and the first wave of 80 million boomers began drawing Social Security in 2008. Retirees *spend less* on goods and services, which means less money in the economy, but they *spend more* on healthcare, which means bigger payouts for government-backed, and tax-funded, Medicare and Medicaid. It's a double whammy to the solar plexus that will weigh down the economy for the next four decades.

Creative Destruction: New and creative uses of technology, led by the Internet, are destroying old industries at a fever pace: Newspapers, magazines, book publishing, the music industry, movie rentals—the list goes on and on—are losing customers and laying off workers by the millions. When 10,000 reporters earning $50,000 a year are laid off, they'll be lucky to earn $5,000 a year blogging on the Internet. That's just one example from one industry. Multiply that by millions of workers in dozens of industries, and all 50 states start to resemble Michigan—high unemployment and lower wages. Even government jobs aren't safe. With the growing popularity of e-mail and online bill payment, the U.S. Postal Service is on track to lose $10 billion in 2009. With salaries accounting for 80% of postal costs, huge layoffs are inevitable.

Peak Oil: Experts agree that we've already extracted half of the world's oil supply, and it will cost more to tap the remaining reserves, which are deeper and harder to reach. Demand, meanwhile, keeps increasing. Millions of products use petroleum as a key ingredient, everything from asphalt to plastic bottles to fertilizer. Trucks and air freight guzzle gas and oil to get those products to market. And the 3 billion upwardly mobile people in China and India will be buying more cars, using more oil, and pumping more gas. More people vying for less oil means prices will go up, up, up, which means consumers will have less discretionary money to spend.

Less Income, More "Needs": Adjusted for inflation, wages continue to go down while people's "needs" continue to soar: A family of four, for example, "needs" four cell phones... at least two, perhaps three cars... GPS systems for the cars... high-speed Internet access... several laptop computers... software and service for those computers... and basic cable TV, at minimum. All these modern-day needs add $200 to $400 to monthly expenses. Meanwhile, companies that used to pay

43

for health insurance and pension plans are transferring those costs to workers, adding another $500 to $1,000 to monthly expenses. What's left over to spend on your wants after paying for all your new needs? We'll be spending nickels and dimes tomorrow on the things we spent dollars on yesterday, causing the economy to slump even more.

Savings Rate Increases: For the decade leading up to the Perfect Recession, the savings rates of Americans averaged a paltry 1%, compared to 20% for the citizens of Japan, China, and India. As recently as the 1980s, the annual savings rate in America was 12%. In 2009, it surged 7% as Americans woke up and started weaning themselves from a 25-year spending binge. For families, increased savings is good. But when the entire nation decides at the same time to increase savings 6%, it takes a big bite out of the economy. How big? Economist Gary Shilling, who predicted the bursting of the housing bubble, thinks a decade-long shift from consumption to savings could take 30% a year out of the economy for the next 10 years. Even if it's half that, it's still huge.

Increasing Healthcare Costs: Healthcare costs are 20% of the gross domestic product—and climbing. In 2009, it cost the average American company $14,000 per year to insure workers and their families. Meanwhile, growing obesity in the general population and an aging population mean more demands for medical treatment at the same time that costs are escalating. As more and more employers shift those costs to consumers, that leaves less money to spend at restaurants, stores, malls, theme parks—they'll all take a hit in the coming decade. Nationalizing healthcare will only make matters worse, as Washington will be forced to increase taxes to pay for their plan, reducing discretionary spending even more.

Under-Funded Pensions: A recent study of 59 state pensions revealed there's a $200 billion shortfall between assets and obligations. To complicate matters, salaries and pensions for the public sector are more generous than those in the private sector. According to the U.S. Labor Department, state and local government employees make 25% more than the average pay of their counterparts in private businesses. Teachers, police, and firefighters typically receive in retirement 80% of their average salary based on their final three years of work. After 30 years, Tampa firefighters earning $80,000 a year would receive 95% of their highest salaries in retirement, meaning a 52-year-old retired firefighter could receive $76,000 a year, plus 3% annual cost-of-living raises, for life. That calculates to a lifetime payout of $2.5 million per retiree. When pensions are under-funded, guess who makes up the difference? You, the taxpayer.

Debt, Debt, and More Debt: Not all debt is bad—getting a loan to start a business or buy investment property is good debt. But racking up consumer debt on credit cards and home equity loans to buy big-screen TVs and book 10-day trips to Disney for the whole family—that's not just bad debt, that's dumb debt. But millions of Americans did just that. The typical American family pays $400 a month just to service their credit cards, whose balances average $11,000 per household. It will take 12 years of $400 monthly payments to eliminate that $11,000 debt, which comes to $60,000. That's $60,000 that could be spent on college for the kids... seed capital to start a new business... or pump up a retirement account. As if consumers weren't strapped enough, home-price declines have left 30% of homeowners with mortgage debt that exceeds the value of their homes. If it's any consolation, corporations aren't in any better shape than consumers. Like most of America, companies borrowed too much and spent too freely. The result: Big, famous-name companies are defaulting on their debts. GM and Chrysler declared bankruptcy in 2009. Other household names to follow: Saks, Century 21 and Coldwell Banker Realty, Blockbuster, American Airlines, Eddie Bauer, and Hilton Hotels. More are sure to follow.

RESPONDING TO THE RESETTING

Is there a way out of this mess... a way to *reset the resetting* so that you and your family are spared a bleak future of high unemployment, high taxes, and low wages? Is there a vessel that can navigate through the Perfect Recession, allowing us to reclaim the American Dream?

Sure is.

The solution, for both you and the country, is for Americans to reconnect with their heritage, to return to the purpose for which the country was colonized, to embrace *entrepreneurship*, the economic force that transformed America from a land of uncultivated prairies and primeval forests to the most prosperous nation in history. Entrepreneurship—it transformed us 400 years ago... and it can transform us once again.

FACED WITH A CHOICE

America is at a crossroad... and Americans are faced with a choice between two promises: On the one hand, we can choose to fulfill the *promise given by our founders*—the promise that in this country, people have the opportunity to become *entrepreneurs*... to succeed or fail of their own volition... to own their own life by owning their own business.

That promise is still available to us.

Or, we can choose the *promise given by big government*, the promise of *entitlements*, the promise that the government will protect us from failure by replacing risk with a safety net...

the promise to make everyone equal by making our salaries the same... our ambitions the same... and our dreams the same.

Sadly, more and more Americans are choosing the promise of big government. To learn why entitlements are the greatest single danger to a vibrant, growing economy, turn the page.

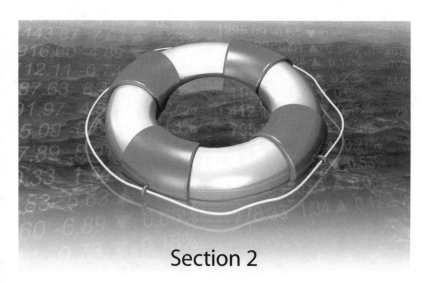

Section 2

The Promises

America is too great for small dreams.

—Ronald Reagan

Entitlements Become Expectations

The Golden Age of Entitlements was 1933 to 1939, when Franklin Roosevelt used the Great Depression as an excuse to usher in dozens of New Deal Programs.

But in the 70-plus years since FDR created the modern welfare state, many government programs started with good intentions during the Great Depression have become bloated entitlements that do more harm than good.

Chapter 3

Entitlements Become Expectations

*The nine most terrifying words
in the English language are:
"I'm from the government,
and I'm here to help."*
—Ronald Reagan

When political thinker and historian Alexis De Tocqueville visited the United States in the 1830s, he praised the American people's love for democracy but cautioned citizens to be wary of democracy's Achilles' heel: *"Any republic will endure until Congress discovers that it can bribe the public with the public's money."*

Unfortunately, that's exactly what has happened over the years as a country *founded on free trade and entrepreneurship* is on the verge of bankrupting itself by offering too many *entitlements* to too many citizens. The result is an unsustainable national debt that keeps piling up, threatening to suffocate our economy and penalize our children and grandchildren with punitive taxes to pay for today's uncontrolled spending.

ENTITLEMENTS SOON BECOME EXPECTATIONS

Most entitlements start off as good intentions—or at least politicians paint them with the brush of good intentions. But once an *entitlement* is in place, it quickly becomes an *expectation* for the people receiving it. Entitlements are easy to give away but impossible to take away. Once they are legislated, and once a segment of the voting public starts enjoying the benefits of those entitlements, they will fight like a cornered badger to preserve them.

The Golden Age of Entitlements was 1933 to 1939, when Franklin Roosevelt used the Great Depression as an excuse to usher in dozens of New Deal programs with the purpose of protecting citizens from the "hazards and vicissitudes of life," to use FDR's words. For sure, some good legislation was passed during FDR's four terms. Prior to 1933, for example, if a bank went bust, investors lost all their money. After the passage of the Federal Deposit Insurance Corporation (FDIC) legislation, the U.S. government has backed 100% of investors' deposits up to $100,000, expanded to $250,000 for 2009. Thousands of banks and savings and loans have failed since 1933, but not a single investor in an FDIC-backed institution has lost so much as a nickel. That's an example of good, lasting legislation.

And to be fair, many social programs enacted during the Great Depression—such as Social Security, unemployment benefits, and welfare—kept thousands from starving when unemployment hit 25% and the economy remained moribund for more than a decade.

But remember, *entitlements become expectations*, and in the 70-plus years since FDR created the modern welfare state, vote-hungry Congress has kept "bribing the public with the public's money" by expanding entitlements. What started out as good intentions has gradually morphed into bloated entitlements that often do more harm than good.

UNINTENDED CONSEQUENCES

Welfare is a classic example of good intentions gone bad.

Welfare and Aid to Families with Dependent Children (AFDC) were birthed during the Social Security Act of 1935. At a time when tens of thousands of children were undernourished and suffering from stunted growth and diseases caused by malnutrition, welfare and AFDC made good sense.

Although the nation has prospered for more than 50 years following WWII, ushering millions of Americans into the middle class, welfare and AFDC kept increasing until they totaled *$24 billion a year* in 1996. Why were millions still stuck in a cycle of poverty when the majority of Americans were doing so well? Because a growing number of unskilled, uneducated women discovered that the U.S. government would reward them for having children out of wedlock by providing monthly checks, subsidized housing, and food stamps.

Talk about an unintended consequence—a government program that was designed to help single mothers and their children had the opposite effect, harming them and their illegitimate offspring by rewarding social dysfunction. As a result, entire generations became dependent on welfare, perpetuating a cycle that has stilted ambition and impoverished several generations of children.

The passage of Minimum Wage legislation in 1938 is yet another example of ill-advised New Deal legislation that continues to haunt us today. Minimum wages were supposed to help lift the "working man" out of poverty by guaranteeing a wage that could support a family. Sounds good on paper—who wouldn't want to help poor people pay their bills and feed their families? Instead, it had the opposite effect. Cash-strapped companies laid off workers and stopped hiring, which increased unemployment and prolonged the Great Depression by several years.

Ironically, the same thing is happening today in the greatest economic downturn since the Great Depression. In the summer of 2009, the minimum wage adjusted to $7.25 an hour from $5.15 per hour in 2007, the largest two-year jump in history. Businesses have responded as they did during FDR's presidency—by laying off thousands of low-skilled workers and putting a freeze on new hires. Some economists claim the unemployment rate would be 50% lower if the minimum wage returned to 2007 levels.

Good intentions. Bad consequences.

ENTITLEMENTS BALLOON YEAR AFTER YEAR

When FDR pushed through dozens of entitlement programs, they represented a small portion of the federal budget. But each year for the past 70-plus years, vote-hungry politicians have kept expanding entitlements until today, the U.S. government spends 20% of the GDP on entitlement programs. By the year 2050, that figure is on track to become 50%.

When a government spends half its revenue on programs for people who are, for the most part, siphoning off wealth instead of creating wealth, then it sets up a system that penalizes the "makers" at the expenses of the "takers."

Take a look at the evolution of the entitlement programs started under FDR's reign:

1. The Works Progress Administration (WPA) subsidized unemployed writers and artists in the '30s and '40s. In 1965, the WPA was replaced by the National Endowment for the Arts, which, in the '80s and '90s, with an annual budget of $100 million, funded obscene and/or heretical "art" exhibits in major museums across the country.

2. The Agricultural Adjustment Administration was formed in 1933 to reduce surpluses that kept prices so low that small farmers couldn't pay their mortgages; the AAA paid farmers NOT to plant some fields. Today, U.S. farmers, including multi-national corporations that own millions of acres of prime farmland, receive $5 billion a year in subsidies for not planting crops.

3. The Social Security Act of 1935 was created as a national pension system for the elderly, when the life expectancy was age 61. Today, the first wave of nearly 80 million baby boomers is beginning to take their benefits at age 62 when their life expectancy is 81, meaning the typical retiree will take out $300,000 to $400,000 during their retirement years, 10 times more than they put into the system.

4. In 1935, the Wagner Act gave workers the right to form unions and bargain collectively. By the 1950s, unions controlled all public jobs in every major city across the country, plus the automobile industry. Excessive wages, benefits, and pensions were major contributors to under-funded state and local pension plans and the bankruptcy of GM and Chrysler.

5. In 1965, Lyndon Johnson signed Medicare and Medicaid into law. Modeled after the Social Security system, a long line of presidents dating back to Teddy Roosevelt sought legislation for a national healthcare system. As 80 million baby boomers head into old age, they'll require expensive joint replacements, more drugs, more major surgeries, longer hospital stays, and increasingly expensive treatments for cancer, diabetes, and heart disease. Bottom line: Skyrocketing Medicare costs will erode the prosperity of at least two younger generations that must pay for the failing health of one older generation, laying the foundation for generational warfare.

ENTITLEMENTS: THE BIGGEST RISK TO RECOVERY

The greatest risk to our recovery comes not from external forces, but from our own growing dependence on the government to solve all our problems. Gary Becker, award-winning economist, describes the threat this way:

The more you have dependence on the government, the more people relying on entitlements become an interest group wanting to maintain those entitlements. The government is spending—at the federal, state, and local level—a 33% of our GDP, and that share is going up. The higher it is, the more people who are directly or indirectly dependent on the government. I am worried about that. Nothing is better at raising productivity, reducing poverty, improving health, and integrating people into the world than the market economy. But entitlements threaten to suffocate free markets with taxes and laws and giveaways. Once entitlements are too ingrained in a government, it is very hard to go back. That's why it's so hard to get any major reform in reducing government spending in Scandinavia and is increasingly so in the United States.

As Steve Forbes, editor-in-chief of *Forbes* magazine reminds us, "Government spending does not create prosperity. If it did, the Soviet Union would have won the Cold War."

ENTITLEMENTS STARVE THE GOLDEN GOOSE

Capitalism, best expressed in entrepreneurship, has been this country's golden goose since the colonial period. The British, French, and Spanish colonized North America with the purpose of growing crops, starting businesses, and expanding trade.

"The business of America is business," President Calvin Coolidge was fond of saying. He was right on the money. Business was the reason the colonies were founded... the reason the colonists declared their independence from England... and the reason we have prospered like no other nation in history.

But entitlements are threatening to put an end to that prosperity.

Entitlements are stealing more and more food from the goose to give to the less productive part of the population. Starve the goose, and you not only kill the goose, you kill the entire country.

And that's exactly what has happened as entitlements are becoming expectations and turning America from a nation of entrepreneurs who *make wealth*... into a nation of entitled citizens who *take wealth*. The post-New Deal mentality of

"You-Got-Yours, So-Where's-Mine?" is starving the golden goose of capitalism by imposing higher taxes and more financial demands on business owners to support social programs, likely soon to include a nationalized healthcare system.

DECLARE YOUR INDEPENDENCE BEFORE IT'S TOO LATE

If we don't want to turn the Perfect Recession into a Permanent Recession, then we need less *entitlement growth* and more *personal growth*. We need to warn people away from entitlements—they dull ambition, reward sloth, discourage risk-taking, and destroy dreams.

I don't want any part of any of those things, do you?

Entitlements aren't the American way.

Entitlements are the weak-willed way.

Entitlements breed dependence on government.

If I'm not mistaken, 233 years ago our Founders signed a Declaration of *Independence*, not a Declaration of *Dependence*.

There's a nearby country where the founder did sign a Declaration of Dependence. The people went along with the founder, choosing government entitlements over entrepreneurship. The citizens depend on the government for everything. Housing. Food. Education. Employment. Healthcare. Everything.

That country is Cuba.

Cuba has entitlements for entrepreneurs, too. Two entitlements, in fact: poverty and prison. So, let's choose entrepreneurship over entitlements in America before it's too late.

Releasing Your Inner Entrepreneur

Government bureaucrats love to dole out dollars. Not their own money, mind you, but money taken from other people. What big government conveniently ignores is that they don't create wealth; they just redistribute wealth created by entrepreneurs.

Instead of waiting around for the government's stimulus package to revitalize the economy, why not create your own stimulus package by starting your own business?

Chapter 4

Releasing Your Inner Entrepreneur

Entrepreneurs are the forgotten
heroes of America.
—Ronald Reagan

As I write this, there are 15 million people out of work, making this the worst job market in a generation. And if you count all the people who have given up trying to find work... are seriously underemployed... are homeless or surviving on a government entitlement... or took early retirement, we're in the worst job market since the Great Depression.

What do you do if you're out of work or stressed because you think your job may be next?

Answer: "Create your own job." So says Jeff Hoffman, founder of Priceline.com and online auctions RedTag.com and UBid.com. "Don't put your dreams on hold just because the economy is bad," Hoffman continues. "During a downturn, there are more opportunities than ever because there are more problems than usual. Help people solve their problems, and you can solve your cash-flow problems."

NOT TO RISK IS TO RISK

When Jim Collins, author of the mega-bestseller *Good to Great*, was teaching business classes at Stanford, he said his students would approach him and say they'd really like to start their own business but weren't ready to take on so much risk.

"You're not ready for risk?" Collins would ask sarcastically. "What's the first thing you learn about investing? Never put all your eggs in one basket. When you take a job, you've just put all your eggs in one basket that is being carried by someone else."

If your employer drops the basket (or more likely in this economy, tosses it out the window), you're going to end up like Humpty Dumpty.

What's the solution? Start your own business.

"As an entrepreneur," Collins continues, "you know what the risks are. You can see them. You understand them. You can manage them. If you work for someone else's company, the risks are still there. But you can't see the risks, and so you can't manage them."

It's only natural for people to avoid risks. But to live is to risk. You drive to work, you risk dying in a car accident. You work at a job, you risk getting laid off. You go on a family ski vacation, you risk breaking a leg. You can't avoid risks, but you can put yourself in situations that minimize risks and allow you to manage them.

The New Deal legislation of the 1930s sought to mitigate risks through government entitlements, but in the long run, all it did was foster more and more dependency on the government. As I said at the end of the previous chapter, the last time I looked, this country was founded on a Declaration of Independence from a tyrannical government, not a Declaration of *Dependence* on a "Daddy Daycare" government.

In the Declaration of *Independence*, we are promised "life, liberty, and the *pursuit* of happiness;" In the Declaration of *Dependence*, we're promised entitlements to a "life of leisure, license, and the pursuit of healthcare."

That sound you hear is our founding fathers turning over in their graves.

NO ENTREPRENEURSHIP, NO RECOVERY

Government bureaucrats love to dole out dollars. Not their own money, mind you, but money taken from other people. What big government conveniently ignores is that they don't *create* wealth; they just *redistribute* wealth created by entrepreneurs.

Unfortunately, at a time when we need entrepreneurs the most, they are hardest to find.

Lifelong entrepreneur Carl Schramm, author of *The Entrepreneurial Imperative*, writes that America's greatness stems from our unparalleled skill as entrepreneurs. The early immigrants came to America to start businesses, not to receive handouts. According to Schramm, "Entrepreneurship alone, not anything else, can give America the necessary leverage to remain an economic superpower."

Unfortunately, at this point in our nation's history, the Entitlement Economy is preempting the Entrepreneurial Economy, according to Schramm:

"I watch the number of new businesses being formed, typically 700,000 a year," Schramm says. "We'll be lucky this year [2009] if it's half that. Almost all new U.S. jobs created come from firms less than five years old. No entrepreneurs, no recovery."

CREATE YOUR OWN STIMULUS PACKAGE BY WORKING FOR YOURSELF

"No entrepreneurs, no recovery" applies to households just as much as to nations. Instead of waiting around for the government's stimulus package to revitalize the economy, why not create your own stimulus package by starting your own business? I know, I know, you're thinking a recession is not the time to be starting a business.

That's where you're wrong. Right now there's a surplus of talented, ambitious people sitting on the sidelines, either unemployed or underemployed, eager for an opportunity to own their own lives by owning their own business. They need to quit making excuses and get back into the game by starting businesses.

"This is a great time to start a recession-resistant business," says Gary Green, author of *No Guts, No Glory* and owner of dozens of franchises in different sectors of the economy. "When people are losing jobs, when you are having to start over at 40 or 50 years old, at what point do you say, 'Enough is enough' and take control of your future?"

I can relate. Back in 1986, I resigned from my teaching job in Illinois and moved to Florida to start a business. When I was teaching, it seemed everyone controlled my life but me. The superintendent told me at which school I would teach. The principal told me what classes I would teach. And the department head told me what classroom I'd teach in.

I figured the only way to take control of my life was to own my own business. So, I resigned from teaching after 18 years in the classroom and headed to Tampa, Florida. I had no business experience. I had no contacts. But I had an eye for opportunity, an open mind, a willingness to learn and work, and a burning desire to own my own life by owning my own business.

It's the best decision I ever made.

Today I own two profitable businesses—a publishing company and a real estate investment company. I work out of a home office, using nothing more than a computer, a three-in-one copier/scan/fax machine, two checkbooks, a well-stocked bookcase, and a calendar. That's really all anyone needs to operate a home-based business. I set my own hours. Choose my own projects. Do my own bookkeeping. And make my own decisions. I wouldn't have it any other way.

TRENDS ARE PUSHING YOU TOWARD SELF-EMPLOYMENT

I understand why most people hesitate to start their own businesses. I was nervous, too, when I started out. But the benefits so outweighed the risks that I jumped in with both feet.

Now, don't get me wrong—I'm not recommending you quit your job and go into business for yourself. That's too risky for most people, especially if you have a family to support. The best time to start a business is on the side, when you already have a full-time job. As W. Randall Jones writes in *The Richest Man in Town: The Twelve Commandments of Wealth*, "Get addicted to ambition, fail to succeed. But most important, keep thy day job."

Many businesses are almost forcing workers to start their own businesses by cutting workers' hours and overtime to save money. In July of 2009, the average work week in the U.S. hit 33 hours, the lowest on record since the government started compiling data 45 years ago. That's bad news for hourly workers but good news for people who want to start a part-time business—it just gives you more time to build a part-time business into a full-time career.

Another trend encouraging self-employment is the increasing number of independent contractors. Businesses don't want to be saddled with paying employees' healthcare, funding retirement plans, and contributing to Social Security. So, they're turning to independent contractors to perform the jobs formerly assigned to employees.

The numbers tell the tale. In *The Future of Work*, a special feature in *Time* magazine, reported that in 10 years, 40% of the workforce will be independent contractors, an increase of 50% from 2009, when 26% of the work force were independent contractors. The article concludes with this statement about changing values in the workplace: "In 10 years, success will be defined not by rank or seniority but by getting what matters to you personally."

WHAT REALLY MATTERS TO ENTREPRENEURS

When I resigned from teaching and started my first business, my biggest motivation wasn't to make more money, although I've certainly done that. When I quit teaching in 1986, I had a doctorate in English, 18 years' experience, and was making a whopping $22,000 a year. I've had single weeks as a publisher and real estate investor when I made that or more.

Although I've had the good fortune to make more money than I ever dreamed possible, my biggest motivation was, and still is, freedom. Freedom from a boss. Freedom to set my own hours. Freedom to pick my own projects. Freedom to call my own shots. Freedom to fail and to learn from those failures. After being on my own for nearly 25 years, I can't imagine working for someone. I'm unemployable and proud of it.

I think most entrepreneurs are like me—they're motivated by more than just money. Certainly money is a biggie. It's the biggest motivator for most people, but certainly not the only motivator. During my discussions with business owners from all sectors of the economy, I've identified the six key motivations for owning your own business. I call these the "Six Top Freedoms of Entrepreneurship." We'll start with financial freedom, because that's the most obvious one. But that doesn't mean it will be *your* top motivation. You go into business for your own reasons, not for someone else's reasons.

Take a look at the list and number them according to your priority.

SIX TOP FREEDOMS OF ENTREPRENEURSHIP

#_____ Freedom to improve your *finances*

#_____ Freedom to control your *fate*

#_____ Freedom to have a *flexible schedule*

#_____ Freedom to have *fun at work*

#_____ Freedom to *fail*

#_____ Freedom for more *family time*

If I were numbering this list, I'd have finances at the very bottom, with *fate* first, followed by *flexible schedule, fun, family time,* and *failure.* But believe me, I've taken advantage of all of these freedoms over the years, including failing. You've likely heard business owners and CEOs of big companies and even top athletes and coaches say they learned more from their failures than from their successes. It's true. There's nothing like pain to drive home a lesson that you need to learn.

DUST OFF YOUR DREAMS

The U.S. is a nation of entrepreneurs. It's woven into our culture. It's part of our genetic makeup, passed down to us from immigrants who had risk-taking typed deep into their DNA.

I mean this literally. Most Americans are descended from people who left their homelands, mostly in Europe, to seek opportunity 3,000 miles away. The cautious people stayed back home, too timid to cut the ties with their way of life. They may have been poor and miserable, but at least it was a misery they were acquainted with. So, the fearful villagers stayed behind while the bold ones boarded ships sailing for America.

It was the daring, adventurous ones—the entrepreneurs —who sought freedom and opportunity in a new land offering a new promise of entrepreneurship to the masses. The ones who immigrated dared to dream of a new and better life.

I believe that all of us who are descended from immigrants carry the same dream in our DNA. We may deny the dream that resides deep inside, but in our quiet, reflective moments, we allow ourselves to dream about being our own boss and making our own way in the world.

"You're not old until regrets take the place of dreams," said the legendary actor John Barrymore. So dust off your dreams before regrets take up permanent residence in your future.

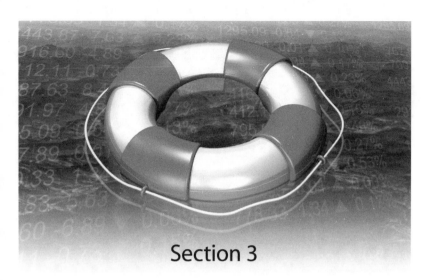

Section 3

The Solution

*It is not the best and brightest
who succeed but those who are
given opportunities and have the
presence of mind to seize them.*

—Malcolm Gladwill,
from *The Outliers: The Story of Success*

The Return to the "Real" American Dream

The American Dream is, first and foremost, about freedom. But in the go-go '80s and '90s, some people's values got high-jacked by the high life, and the concept of FREEDOM got pushed aside by STARDOM.

For some Americans, the American Dream became less about freedom and more about fame and fortune AT ANY COST, even if it meant lying and cheating to get it.

Chapter 5

The Return to the "Real" American Dream

*Everything that is really great
and inspiring is created by the
individual who can labor in freedom.*
—Albert Einstein

In today's global economy, manufacturing can't support the American middle class anymore. How can we compete with Chinese and Vietnamese workers who will happily work 10-hour days in a manufacturing plant for 60 cents an hour?

Answer: We can't.

Because emerging markets can make things 100 times cheaper than the U.S., foreign manufacturers will continue to dominate the old *Material Economy*. But in the new *Mental Economy*, where brains win out over brawn, the U.S. can still reign supreme.

We may not be able to *out-cheap* them, but...

We can *out-think* them.

We can *out-innovate* them.

We can *out-service* them.

We can *out-market* them.

Oh, and one other thing—we can *out-dream* them.

Big achievements start with big dreams, and big dreamers in America showed the world the way to democracy... won world wars... and put men on the moon. It took money to accomplish these dreams, but it wasn't money that motivated men to face down machine gun fire and storm the beaches of Normandy in WWII.

It was freedom.

THE EVOLUTION OF THE AMERICAN DREAM

We Americans are unique in having a national dream.

There is no French Dream. Or German Dream. Or Chinese Dream. Or Canadian Dream, even though we share a continent and basic values with our neighbor to the north.

The American Dream is our birthright, born by the Declaration of Independence... nursed by free enterprise... and nurtured by opportunities for the masses. By offering commoners the opportunity for freedom, dignity, and, yes, financial prosperity (without which real freedom could not exist), the American Dream unlaced the societal straight jackets imposed by social class and caste systems that dominated the rest of the world. As a result, millions fled their oppressive homelands and sailed for the New World.

Although the spirit of the American Dream has been around for four centuries, the actual term "the American Dream" is less than 100 years old, first popularized by James Adams in his book *The Epic of America*, published in 1931. In the book, Adams defines our cultural yearning as "... that American Dream of a better, richer, and happier life for all our citizens of every rank... one in which the common man as well as the leader was hoping for greater *freedom* and happiness for himself and his children."

Ah, there's that word again—*freedom*—the heart and soul of the American Dream. What kind of freedom did immigrants flock to America seeking? The best description of freedom can be traced to Franklin Roosevelt's 1941 State of the Union address when he cited the "four essential human freedoms" that the U.S. would be fighting for in WWII:

FOUR ESSENTIAL HUMAN FREEDOMS
1) Freedom of speech and expression
2) Freedom of every person to worship God in his own way
3) Freedom from fear
4) Freedom from want

Stirred by these words, Norman Rockwell, the great American artist, painted his Four Freedoms series, reproduced in 1943 by the *Saturday Evening Post.* The paintings proved so popular that the Office of War organized a national tour featuring the original works, raising $133 million in war bonds at packed venues.

NEVER TAKE FREEDOM FOR GRANTED
The true meaning of the American Dream—and the true meaning of freedom—can be summed up in the life of Ben Steele, a retired 92-year-old art professor and survivor of the infamous Bataan Death March.

In 1942, the Japanese forced 76,000 American soldiers and captured Filipinos to march 60 miles in the tropical heat without food and water to a slave labor camp. Steele spent three years in the camp, surviving on a small bowl of watery rice each day amid frequent beatings and rampant outbreaks of malaria and dysentery.

Retired for two decades, Steele starts each morning with a short walk to his art studio 100 feet from the house he's owned for 40 years. He spends his morning sketching memories of his internment in the Philippines, which are still vivid in his memory 70 years later. Steele says the best part of his day begins the moment he walks out his back door to the studio:

"I'm free," he exclaims. "I go where I want. I do what I want to do. It's wonderful."

Ben Steele knows what it feels like to lose the American Dream, if only for three years in a rat-infested jungle harassed day and night by sadistic guards. Unlike most Americans who take freedom for granted, Ben Steel understands what the real American Dream is all about.

It's about freedom.

And it's wonderful.

THE DARK SIDE OF THE AMERICAN DREAM

Despite what is depicted on the glammed-up reality TV shows, the essence of the American Dream isn't stardom or bling or gaudy-excess success. The American Dream is, first and foremost, about freedom.

The freedom to own your own life by owning your own business. The freedom to be your own boss… set your own hours… choose when you work and with whom you work—that's true freedom. That's why I say freedom, not money, is the heart and soul of the American Dream.

Don't misunderstand. Money is important. Money is good. But when money becomes a person's Mammon, the false god of riches, then good values get replaced by greed, and unbridled worshipers of money will go to any lengths, justify any means, to acquire money, even if it means cheating, lying, and scheming to get it.

And that's just what happened in the go-go '80s and '90s, when some people's values got high-jacked by the high life, and the concept of FREEDOM (the right to determine your own destiny) got pushed aside by STARDOM (the desire to show off their assets, both physical and material). The American Dream became, for some Americans, less about freedom and more about *fame and fortune*—at any cost.

CAPITALISM WITHOUT A CONSCIENCE

In the two decades leading up to the Perfect Recession, some businessmen—too many businessmen, for that matter—lost their moral bearings. They focused solely on making money to the point that the ringing of the cash register drowned out the voices calling for honesty and integrity.

Doing the right thing for the right reasons got replaced by doing whatever it takes to rake in the bucks. All too many people hid their conscience in a vault along with the ill-gotten gains.

I call these people, "Capitalists without a Conscience."

Capitalists without a Conscience can reap some short-term financial gains. Sometimes they even amass huge fortunes. But eventually, their lies and licentiousness catch up with them. As Warren Buffett likes to say, "When the tide goes out, you find out who has been swimming naked."

The tide went out during the Perfect Recession. And the longer the tide stays out, the more scammers and crooks and swindlers and Ponzi schemers we see trudging red-faced back to the beach.

Turn to the next chapter to learn who got exposed as a fraud when the Perfect Recession swept across our economy.

Capitalists **<u>WITHOUT</u>** a Conscience

*Capitalism will always have a few
crooks and conmen who profit from
others' pain. These "Capitalists
Without a Conscience" line
their pockets at the expense
of innocent people.*

*A favorite con game of Capitalists
Without a Conscience is the Ponzi
scheme—an illegal pyramid that
pays founders and early investors
out-sized returns from the money
of later investors. Bernie Madoff
was the king of Ponzi schemers, but
the Perfect Recession blew the cover
off dozens of pyramid schemes all
across North America*

Pyramid Schemes: Capitalists without a Conscience

A man who has never gone
to school may steal from a
freight car, but if he has a
university education, he may
steal the whole railroad.
—Teddy Roosevelt

There's an old adage that sums up the basic difference between socialism and capitalism:

The problem with socialism is socialism (the system itself is flawed).

The problem with capitalism is CAPITALISTS (some individuals within the system are flawed).

And boy, oh, boy, have we had some problem capitalists lately. There must be one on every corner of Manhattan these days.

I call the crooks and con artists who operate in the dark corners of capitalism *Capitalists without a Conscience*. They line their own pockets at the expense of innocent people. Capitalism will always have a few capitalists who profit from others' pain. But during the Perfect Recession, the canvas covering these Capitalists without a Conscience was blown off, revealing a parade of Ponzi schemers, led by the prince of the Ponzi scheme, Bernie Madoff.

ILLEGAL PYRAMID SCHEMES: YESTERDAY AND TODAY

The Ponzi scheme—also known as a pyramid scheme—gets its name from Carlos "Charles" Ponzi, who enticed investors back in the 1920s with promises of 50% gains in a few months' time. Early on, Ponzi could pay outsized gains to early investors because tons of money was coming into the base of the pyramid-shaped investment structure from later investors, while a smaller amount of money was being funneled up to the early investors (and Ponzi himself) at the top.

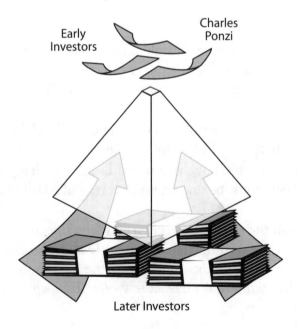

Illegal Pyramid Scheme

Early Investors

Charles Ponzi

Later Investors

As long as investors could crow about their big returns, the pyramid appeared legitimate. But when newspapers exposed Ponzi as a crook, the flow of new money stopped, and thousands of furious investors demanded their money back. But they quickly discovered the money was gone, paid out to early investors or stolen by Ponzi to support his extravagant lifestyle. As the police closed in, Ponzi's illegal pyramid collapsed like a house of cards.

I suppose you could excuse people in the 1920s for falling for a Ponzi scheme. Back then, people were less educated. Many immigrants in big cities were illiterate or couldn't speak English. There was no TV. There was no Securities and Exchange Commission overseeing the markets, so it was much easier for *Capitalists without a Conscience* to "cook the books."

But a Ponzi scheme could *never* happen nowadays in the Information Age, what with 24/7 Internet access to information coupled with government watchdog agencies overseeing investment houses, right?

Wrong.

Flash forward 80 years to December 10, 2008. For much of the year, the stock market has been falling like rain in a monsoon, and anxious investors in Madoff Investment Securities were seeking to withdraw $7 billion. The founder and namesake of the nearly 50-year-old company, Bernie Madoff, confessed to his two sons that the company didn't have billions because Madoff had been running a Ponzi scheme for decades.

Madoff scammed 13,500 investors out of $65 billion during the course of his pyramid scheme. Meanwhile, he and his wife lived the life of luxury, with a $24 million private jet, two yachts, and homes in Manhattan, Palm Beach, and France. Among the scammed were retirees, supposed best friends, and scores of charities, some of which had to close their doors after learning Madoff had spent their endowment money. Madoff is truly a *Capitalist without a Conscience*.

But he had plenty of company.

A ROGUES' GALLERY OF PONZI SCHEMERS

Madoff was the Grand Poohbah of Ponzi schemers, but the worst recession in generations has uncovered dozens of other pyramid schemes operated by *Capitalists without a Conscience*. Here are a few of the boldest and least-principled Ponzi punks:

- In New York, Marc Dreier, a high-profile lawyer, sold investors $700 million in fictitious promissory notes to support a lavish lifestyle, including a vast art collection adorning the walls of his Manhattan penthouse.

- In Sarasota, Florida, Richard Piccoli, an 82-year-old businessman, pleaded guilty to running a Ponzi scheme from 2002 to 2009, stealing $31 million from clients he recruited largely from ads in Catholic newspapers and from his membership in the Knights of Columbus, the world's largest Catholic fraternal organization.

- Back in Manhattan, Mark Bloom, founder of a bogus hedge fund, is awaiting trial for diverting $20 million of investors' money to his personal accounts to buy a $5 million triplex in prestigious Gracie Square, a fleet of foreign cars, assorted boats, a beach house, topped off with his spending $300,000 on his daughter's bat mitzvah.

- In Canada, Frederick Elliott and his son, Derek, a pair of real estate developers, swindled 1,600 private

U.S. investors out of $170 million in a pyramid scheme they set up to pay for, among other things, a failed resort in the Dominican Republic, lavish family shopping sprees, a private plane, a yacht, and a country music tour bus.

• In Antigua by way of Houston, Allen Stanford vaulted onto the *Forbes* list of the 400 richest Americans, amassing an $8 billion Caribbean banking empire and skimming off at least $1 billion for personal use to pay for a 120-foot yacht, a fleet of airplanes, multiple families, a moated Miami mansion, and a $20 million prize paid by Stanford himself to his own cricket team, the Stanford Superstars, for winning the Stanford Super Series. Stanford avoided detection of his Ponzi scheme for years by, among other things, contributing $2.4 million to Republican political campaigns and sponsoring dozens of free "fact-finding" trips to the Caribbean islands for politicians and their staffs on his fleet of jets.

• In New York (no big surprise), Stephen Walsh and Paul Greenwood are charged with operating a pyramid scheme through a phony hedge fund that misappropriated $553 million from universities, public pension funds, and retirement plans to support their lavish lifestyles, including multi-million-dollar homes and a horse farm.

LEGAL PYRAMID SCHEMES

The Ponzi-schemers mentioned above are all headed to prison, and Madoff, for one, will certainly die there, as the 71-year-old confessed crook was sentenced to 150 years in prison.

But there were plenty of other crooks posing as investors, bankers and CEOs during the run up to the Perfect Recession who won't spend so much as a minute for their crimes against American taxpayers because their actions weren't technically illegal.

Unethical, yes. Illegal, no.

What I'm talking about are the overpaid CEOs of public companies and the Wall Street financial wizards who were paid billions in salaries and bonuses prior to the financial meltdown that began in the fall of 2007. Year-end bonuses on Wall Street topped out at $33 billion in 2007, with the average worker pulling down $240,000 after bonuses in 2007. Note—that's the *average salary* for Wall Street workers, which would include secretaries, doormen, runners, and maintenance men. For two decades, everybody working on Wall Street cashed in big before the Perfect Recession blew into town. Yes, EVERYBODY pulled down big bucks, but the few lucky ones at the top of these legal pyramid schemes made absolute fortunes.

The biggest beneficiary of Wall Street bonuses was Richard Fuld, the CEO of Lehman Brothers who steered this 158-year-old investment bank into bankruptcy by placing big bets on subprime mortgages and high-risk financial products. From 2000, when the housing bubble kicked into overdrive, to 2008, when the bubble burst, Fuld received $450 million in compensation.

Stockholders in Lehman prior to 2007 didn't object to Fuld's huge compensation package because Lehman's profits continued to climb steadily upward during Fuld's tenure. But, as we have come to learn, the profits were largely derived from highly leveraged, risky bets on subprime mortgages, and when the real estate bubble burst, so did the profit picture at Lehman.

Here's my question: If Fuld got paid hundreds of millions because he made winning bets using stockholders' money, shouldn't he give back hundreds of millions when those same bets headed south, creating huge losses for Lehman's stockholders and forcing the company into bankruptcy?

Should happen—but it won't.

Fuld, like everyone else on Wall Street who rode the gravy train right up to the bursting of the bubble, got to keep the money he reaped when Wall Street was making hay, but he wasn't penalized like the stockholders and taxpayers were when his reckless driving wrecked the gravy train. Working on Wall Street is like gambling with house money in a casino. When they win big, they take the profits. But when they lose big, the casino (in our case, we taxpayers) covers the losses. Unlike you and me, when titans of Wall Street gambled, it was a "heads-they-win, tails-they-win" proposition.

WALL STREET: LEGAL PYRAMID SCHEME?

In effect, Wall Street has been running a giant **pyramid scheme** longer than Bernie Madoff, who started his firm in 1960. Difference is, Bernie's pyramid scheme was illegal and, technically, Wall Street's wasn't. The public put their money—and their trust—in financial institutions, and the lion's share of that money funneled up to the money managers, traders, dealmakers, and officers of those firms. They made hundreds of billions during the 10 years from 1997 to late 2007, while the stock market lost 3% during the same time frame. The money kept swirling around the Wall Street pyramids, popping out the top into the pockets of the money men in Manhattan while seldom, if ever, making it into the pockets of everyday people.

89

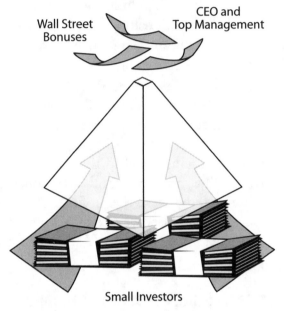

Legal (but Unethical) Pyramid

Wall Street Bonuses

CEO and Top Management

Small Investors

When the music stopped in this money version of musical chairs, the guys and gals at the top of this legal pyramid scheme got another round of bonuses, while the little people at the bottom got a bill for $700 billion in bailout money.

A great deal if you work on Wall Street.

A lousy deal if you work on Main Street.

ALTRUISTIC MARKETING™: YOUR TICKET TO FREEDOM

Okay, we've talked about illegal pyramid schemes and legal pyramid schemes. But does that mean every business or enterprise shaped like a pyramid is automatically a scheme?

That's not the case. Not even close to being true.

Truth is, virtually every organization is shaped like a pyramid, from law firms to lawn-mowing services... from the Boy Scouts to beauty shops... from Subway franchises to subway transportation systems and everything in between.

Pyramids are natural structures for organizing people and processes, so much so that every organization in the world that distributes goods and services or coordinates activities is shaped like a pyramid. It's not the *shape* that determines whether the entity is legitimate or a scheme; it's the *people and the purpose* behind the pyramid that makes it legal or illegal, ethical or unethical.

Capitalists without a Conscience will always find ways to short-circuit capitalism or to rewire the corporate cash register to put more money in their pockets. *Capitalists with a Conscience*, on the other hand, will always operate with honesty and integrity, not because they're afraid of getting caught, but because it's the right thing to do.

There are a few industries, which, by their very mission and function, are virtually self-policing, requiring exceptional honesty and integrity from participants. One such industry is Altruistic Marketing™, a business owned and operated by Capitalists with a Conscience.

Turn the page to learn more.

Altruistic Marketing™:
Capitalists <u>WITH</u> a Conscience

*Like capitalism itself, it's the ethics
and intentions of the capitalists
managing the corporate structure
that make a pyramid good or bad,
a legitimate business or a scheme.*

*Altruistic Marketing™—people
helping themselves by helping others
to help themselves—takes Capitalism
with a Conscience to a whole new
level. Unlike cut-throat capitalism,
Altruistic Marketing™ is a sharing,
caring business built on friendships,
trust, and appreciation.*

Altruistic Marketing™: Capitalists with a Conscience

Man is a knot, a web, a mesh into
which relationships are tied. In
the patter and panorama of life,
only those relationships matter.
—Saint-Exupery,
from *Flight to Arras*

Thank goodness Bernie Madoff's pyramid scheme is the exception, not the rule.

Perhaps you've heard people mistakenly call Referral Marketing or Person-to-Person Marketing—I prefer the term *Altruistic Marketing™*—a "pyramid scheme."

It's time to squelch that rumor once and for all.

LOOK TO THE LEADERS, NOT THE SHAPE

As I said in the previous chapter, it's not the structure itself that makes a pyramid a scheme. In effect, every organization with three or more members is shaped like a pyramid, with a leader or founder at the top and multiple layers that get bigger and wider at the bottom.

Corporate Pyramid

No one calls Wal-Mart and McDonald's pyramid schemes. No one calls the Boy Scouts of America a pyramid scheme. No one calls the Shriners and Kiwanis Clubs pyramid schemes. Yet they all operate in a corporate pyramid structure, with the CEO at the top and the cashiers and/or clerical workers at the bottom.

That's why I tell people *to look to the leaders and the length of time in business*, not the shape. Those two things will tell you whether a company is legitimate or not. An industry can't operate in the open for 60-plus years, as Altruistic Marketing™

has done, and be a scheme. Madoff ran the longest-running pyramid scheme in history, pulling the wool over investors' and the SEC's eyes for 20 years. But operating a pyramid scheme in the open for 60 years without getting busted?

Impossible.

Like capitalism itself, it's the *ethics and intentions* of the capitalists managing the corporate structure, especially the leader at the top, which make a pyramid good or bad, a legitimate business or a scheme.

But to put this rumor to rest once and for all, let's look to noted author and educator Dr. Dean Black as he explains how organizational pyramids operate:

> Delegation creates a pyramid structure. Our government is a many-leveled pyramid. So are our schools and churches. All successful businesses, because they distribute goods and services, end up shaped like a many-leveled pyramid. In any pyramid, the power [or the profits] comes from the bottom. Marketing companies distribute products down a pyramid, but consumers give them money from the bottom. So, pyramids set up a flow that runs both ways: first down, then up. Value flows down the pyramid, money, in response, flows up. If value stops flowing down, then money stops flowing up and the system collapses.

Legal (and Ethical) Business Structure

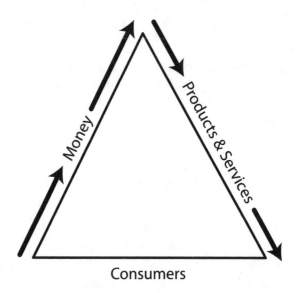

Dr. Black's description explains why pyramid schemes, such as Bernie Madoff's, eventually collapse: When Madoff could no longer push value in the form of dollars down the pyramid because no new money was coming in, then his system collapsed.

But the definition also explains the legitimacy of Altruistic Marketing™. Based on word-of-mouth endorsements—one satisfied customer to another—in the Altruistic Marketing™ model, value in the form of products and services flows down, and in response, money flows up to the marketer and manufacturer. Marketers and companies that don't provide value in exchange for money are illegal scams and attorney's general and the FTC shut them down and march the offenders off to prison quicker than you can say "Pyramid Scheme."

So, a big, big benchmark for the legitimacy of an Altruistic Marketing™ company is how long they've been in business. Companies with a 5... 10... 20... 30... 40... or 50-plus-year history must be legal or they would have been shut down years ago.

OPPORTUNITY: THE ULTIMATE VALUE-ADDED PRODUCT

Because they offer value-added, state-of-the-art products that every household needs and wants *even during recessions* ("household essentials," I call them), Altruistic Marketing™ companies are virtually recession-proof. Household essentials include necessities people have to buy month in and month out, such as optimal nutrition drinks and phytonutrient-based supplements... healthful energy drinks packed with B vitamins and amino acids... technologically superior anti-aging skincare lines... carbohydrate blockers and weight management supplements... eco-friendly laundry and cleaning supplies... and air and water purification systems, to name a few.

But with Altruistic Marketing™, the *ultimate value* flowing down to consumers is *opportunity*—a concept unavailable in traditional wholesale and retail settings. Former college marketing professor, Dr. Bill Quain, calls Altruistic Marketing™ "pro-suming," as it offers consumers the ultimate in added value: "The opportunity for consumers to create income, instead of only out-go, when they shop."

With Altruistic Marketing™, consumers enjoy *twice* the added-value flowing down from the corporation: superior products delivered to their door, PLUS a superior opportunity to create wealth and to pursue the true American Dream, *freedom*, by owning and operating your own home-based business.

99

CAPITALISM WITH A CONSCIENCE

Before I explain why I think Altruistic Marketing™ is the epitome of *Capitalism with a Conscience*, let's take a moment to review the advantages of owning your own business, as well as the different types of businesses available to you.

I, for one, can testify to the enormous advantages of self-employment. I set my own hours, choose my own projects, choose the people I work with, and control my income. The more hours I work and the more books I write and publish, the more money I make. I can't imagine having to ask a boss, perhaps someone half my age, to approve my vacation days. How humiliating!

I've been self-employed since moving to Tampa in 1986. I can tell you from experience that integrity is the cornerstone of every small business—every business, for that matter. People who cut corners or cheat partners and clients don't stay open very long.

That's why I say the only *capitalism that endures is capitalism WITH a conscience*, which means operating with honesty and integrity in your dealings with people. *Capitalists WITHOUT a conscience*, such as the Bernie Madoffs of the world, may operate in the shadows for a while, but eventually, the spotlight of truth shines on the crooks and con men, and they wind up spending a big chunk of their lives in a 6-foot-by-9-foot cinderblock cell with bars on the door.

Listed below are the six basic types of business opportunities available to average entrepreneurs—"average" meaning everyday people like you and me, as opposed to the one-in-a-million genius types who start a billion-dollar business in their garage or college dorm room, like Steve Jobs, Bill Gates, and Michael Dell.

SIX BASIC BUSINESS OPPORTUNITIES
FOR SELF-EMPLOYMENT

1) **Manual Labor:** handyman, house cleaning, yard service; low risk, low reward, low leverage (one hour of work = one hour of pay)

2) **Commission Only Sales:** residential and commercial real estate and contract sales; low up front investment, high return for super-talented, super salespeople, who are rare

3) **Consulting:** low risk, high return, but requires super-smart people with specialized knowledge

4) **Store Owner:** high risk (must lease space and buy inventory) and reasonable reward for one location; multiple locations can mean bigger profits but require a bigger investment

5) **Franchise Owner:** high risk (franchise fees, leased space, and inventory can costs hundreds of thousands of dollars), reasonable return for one location; multiple locations mean bigger income but require a bigger investment; "paint-by-numbers" business plan increases chance of success

6) **Altruistic Marketing:** low risk, potential high reward with a proven, duplicable business model that leverages money, time, and efforts

ALTRUISTIC MARKETING™: CAPITALISM WITH A CONSCIENCE

Most everyone is familiar with the first five types of business opportunities. I've owned and operated the first three types myself—I opened a sole proprietorship in college to paint houses during the summers, started a company to sell environmental products and books on a commission-only basis, and have consulted as part of my book publishing business.

For sure, publishing and my real estate investments have been far more profitable than the others thanks to leverage, which we will talk more about in a moment.

But the sixth type of business opportunity, Altruistic Marketing™, takes *Capitalism with a Conscience* to a whole new level. I define Altruistic Marketing™ as "people helping themselves by helping others help themselves." In Altruistic Marketing™, you make money by making a difference in people's lives. You not only offer products and services that people need, you also offer consumers the opportunity to own a low-cost, potentially high-return business they can start on a shoestring without having to quit their full-time jobs.

Your success in Altruistic Marketing™ depends on your ability to learn the business, then to sponsor and coach others how to succeed. You're rewarded for helping people grow personally and professionally. There's an old saying in this business: "No one cares how much you know until they know how much you care." Unlike cutthroat capitalism, *Capitalism with a Conscience* is a sharing, caring business, built on friendships, trust, and appreciation. Little wonder, then, that recognition of achievements is a favored tradition in this business.

Altruistic Marketing™ is a servant-leader, team-building business. How many businesses can you say that about? Sponsoring partners are rewarded for coaching new people to excel and outperform everyone, even the team leaders. You can't say that about corporate America, can you? Unlike *Capitalism without a Conscious*, Altruistic Marketing™ puts people above profits, for people are the engine that drives the growth of your business.

In this business, people skills and profit skills go hand in hand. In Altruistic Marketing™, you're not just building a business—you're building a community of like-minded people who want to do well for themselves by doing good for others.

Are you beginning to see why I single out Altruistic Marketing™ for being a stellar example of *Capitalism with a Conscience?*

FACTS ABOUT THE INDUSTRY

"Facts are stubborn things," according to Ronald Reagan, so let's take moment to look at the facts about Altruistic Marketing™ to see if it is, indeed, *Capitalism with a Conscience.*

A type of direct selling, Altruistic Marketing™ has been around for 60-plus years. Currently there are 29 direct selling companies traded publicly on stock exchanges around the globe, with 21 of those classified as Altruistic Marketing™ companies.

According to *Prosper* magazine, in 2007, 15 million people across the U.S. distributed about $31 billion worth of products to consumers. Worldwide, direct sales topped $114 billion for 2007. Nearly 33% of the national direct sales force have college degrees, and 10% even have post-graduate degrees.

Best of all, Altruistic Marketing™ is practically recession proof. "Direct selling does very well during recessions," says Amy Robinson, vice president of communications for the Direct Selling Association. "It's a great opportunity for people who have been laid off or who need extra money to make ends meet." In the last three recessions—1990, 1991, and 2001—direct selling grew 30% during the downturns.

During down times, people with an entrepreneurial spirit flock to Altruistic Marketing™. Uber-entrepreneur Donald

Trump sums up the appeal this way: "The industry is attractive to people who want or need to diversify their income. This [the Perfect Recession] is truly a chance for millions of Americans to better their lives."

TIMING COULDN'T BE BETTER

You've likely heard the expression, "Timing is everything in life and business." So true. The timing to get involved in Altruistic Marketing™ couldn't be better, as the biggest opportunities today—and for decades to come—are not in *making products*, which China can do cheaper than the U.S. or Canada, but in *marketing products*.

Unlike in-your-face shock advertising so prevalent today, Altruistic Marketing™ operates on the softer side of capitalism, whereby cooperation... communication... and community take precedence over competition and cut-rate prices.

By distributing technologically superior products that every household needs and consumes regularly, Altruistic Marketers™ offer a hi-touch alternative to a hi-tech world hungry for handshakes and hugs, instead of the soul-deadening diet of TV and text messages.

Jack Welch, former CEO of GE, understands that to be successful in business today, you have to put *people* back in the *marketing picture*: Writing in *BusinessWeek* magazine, Welch puts technology in its proper perspective with these wise words:

> "Relationships matter. Real ones, perhaps maintained electronically, but built the old-fashioned way, person-to-person, and face-to-face. Get to know people. Let them get to know you. Being online is fine, but being there in person is imperative."

"Being there in person is imperative"—that should be the motto of every business in the post-Perfect Recession era. And no business puts people first better than Altruistic Marketing™.

GET ON BOARD A BULL MARKET

When the stock market goes up across the board, it's called a *bull market*. When it goes down, it's called a *bear market*. But even in the worst bear markets, there are always some industries headed upward. During the lowest point of the Perfect Recession, for example, Wal-Mart and low-priced dollar stores saw big jumps in business as cash-strapped consumers were pinching their pennies.

"There's always a bull market somewhere," exclaimed Jim Cramer, successful hedge fund manager and host of MSNBC's *Mad Money*. "And you know what's in a tremendous bull market mode during this recession? Direct selling!"

Because the Perfect Recession is poised to transition into a *permanent resetting*, Altruistic Marketing™ is in the perfect position to attract dormant entrepreneurs and grow for decades to come.

There's a surplus of ambitious, talented people sitting on the sidelines, just waiting for an opportunity to own their own lives by owning their own business.

You may be one of those people.

You have a choice: You can remain sitting on the sidelines and hope the recession recedes and the go-go '90s makes a rip-roaring return in 2010. I wouldn't bet my future on that happening, however. There's a name for that kind of hope. It's called wishful thinking.

Or, you can jump on board an industry that has performed well in recessions and, given the economic trends facing us in the next decade, is certain to attract new talent and grow year in and year out.

As the Perfect Recession sweeps across the continent and the world, you can ride the tidal wave of Altruistic Marketing™ to a bright, new future. Millions of people around the globe are choosing not just to survive, but also to thrive, with Altruistic Marketing™.

Conclusion

Your Moment on the Bridge

In the fall of 2007, the economy went into a tailspin, and the facts about the economy changed. You're faced with a choice: You can run back to the still-smoking ruins of the Perfect Recession, hoping the economy will return to the go-go '90s.

Or, you can run in the direction of your dreams—the REAL American Dream—the dream of owning your own life by owning your own business.

Conclusion

Your Moment on the Bridge

*There is a tide in the
affairs of men,
Which, taken at the flood,
leads on to fortune;
Omitted, all the voyage
of their life
Is bound in shallows and misery.*
—William Shakespeare

On September 11, 2001, a newspaper reporter stood on the Brooklyn Bridge and watched the south tower of the World Trade Center collapse. He could hear police sirens heading toward the bridge in both directions, and, being a seasoned journalist, he knew it was only a matter of minutes before the police closed the bridge.

He only had a moment to make the most important decision of his life.

Should he run back to Brooklyn to protect his wife and child? Or should he dash toward lower Manhattan and risk his life reporting on the biggest story of his life?

The reporter, Rod Dreher, chose the "dull, dutiful thing: to go home and look after my family."

Dreher acknowledges that had he chosen to run toward the disaster instead of home, he would have gotten the story of a lifetime—a story that most reporters never get anywhere near in their entire careers. And here it was, right before his eyes, history in the making only a 10-minute dash away to innumerable bylines... journalism awards... syndicated columns... professional prestige—all of the things ambitious reporters dream about.

He chose the dutiful thing and ran for home.

YOUR TIME TO CHOOSE

Today, right now, is your moment on the bridge. You can run back toward the still-smoking ruins of the Perfect Recession—your job, if it's still there... lower wages... a boss who wants you to perform enough to make him look good but not so much that you'll take his job... longer hours for less money... with only two words standing between you and the street—"you're fired."

Or, you can run toward the real American Dream—freedom through free enterprise—owning your own life by owning your own business and controlling your own fate by building a home-based business through Altruistic Marketing™.

When a reporter asked the legendary economist John Maynard Keynes why he had reversed himself on one of this theories, he replied, *"When the facts change, I change my mind. What about you?"*

Well, in the fall of 2007, the facts changed when the Perfect Storm crashed into Wall Street.

The world economy went into a tailspin, and the ensuing

crash revealed numerous structural problems that led to the worst economic crisis since the Great Depression. It will take time and money to repair the economy—and the go-go '90s are gone forever.

Layoffs are up. Entitlements are up. Unemployment is up. And anxiety is up.

But wages are down. Job opportunities are down. Job security is down. Housing prices are down. Pensions are down. And sadly, even some people's dreams are down.

The facts changed.

Are you willing to change? Willing to open your mind to opportunity? To take a chance on yourself? To change the direction of your life while you still have time? To dare to dream big dreams again?

You're on the bridge. It's time to choose.

Do you choose to *deny* your independence by running in the direction of your past? Or do you choose to *declare* your independence by running in the direction of your dreams?

Millions have chosen to embrace the beauty of the REAL American Dream.

What will *you* choose?